T0208147

MY GRANDMOTHER

MY GRANDMOTHER

An Armenian-Turkish Memoir

FETHIYE ÇETIN

Translated by Maureen Freely

VERSO

London • New York

This paperback edition first published by Verso 2012
First published by Verso 2008
© Verso 2008
Translation © Maureen Freely 2008
Introduction © Maureen Freely 2008
First published as *Anneannem: Anlatı*
© Metis Yayinlari 2004

1 3 5 7 9 10 8 6 4 2

Verso
UK: 6 Meard Street, London W1F 0EG
US: 388 Atlantic Ave, Brooklyn, NY 11217
www.versobooks.com

Verso is the imprint of New Left Books

ISBN-13: 978-1-84467-867-9

British Library Cataloguing in Publication Data
A catalogue record for this book is available from the British Library

Library of Congress Cataloging-in-Publication Data
A catalog record for this book is available from the Library of Congress

Typeset by Hewer Text UK Ltd, Edinburgh
Printed in the US

I would like to thank my dear Ayşe, Nadire, Necmiye, Zeynep, Zehra and Handan, who gave me the courage to write this book, and did everything in their power to help me persevere, casting aside any excuse I made to shirk from the task; if it hadn't been for you, this book would never have come into being. I am so fortunate to know you, and to have you as my friends.

Preface

Maureen Freely

When victorious generals sit down to dictate history, their greatest privilege is to choose what to leave out. Thus, Europeans know little or nothing about the 1920 Treaty of Sèvres, which, had it been ratified, would have carved up most of what was left of the Ottoman Empire at the end of World War One. Izmir and the Aegean coast would have passed to the Greeks; a large part of eastern Anatolia might have become part of an independent Armenia, leaving only Istanbul and northern Anatolia in Ottoman hands. But since much of this region was under Allied occupation in 1920, it, too, had taken on the aspect of a European colony. And so it might have remained, if Mustafa Kemal's armies had not risen up to reclaim the lands that now define the Republic of Turkey.

But in 1927, when Kemal sat down to write the official history of its birth, Sèvres still cast a long shadow. It was the future that might have been, had Europe and Anatolia's Christian minorities had their way. It is through this prism that four generations of Turkish schoolchildren have been taught to view the catastrophes of the last years of the Ottoman Empire, when Anatolia was between one quarter and one third Christian. They are not told that the triumvirate then in charge of the empire wished to 'Turkify' Anatolia by reducing that population to a level that would render it politically insignificant. Nor are they told that the same cadre aimed to relocate and resettle Anatolia's many Muslim minorities – Kurdish, Arab, Circassian, Georgian, Laz, Albanian, Bulgarian, amongst others – with a view to assimilating them. Instead they are told that that the Armenians were fighting alongside the Russians, in the process killing many Muslim Turks. They are also told that the deportations and massacres of 1915 were in response to this treachery, and that diaspora claims that as many as 1.5 million Armenians lost their lives are grossly inflated and motivated mainly by a desire for money and territory.

For the past eighty years, Turkey's powerful army and state bureaucracies have guarded the official history with the greatest zeal. Its penal codes are laden with laws severely curbing free expression, ensuring that most Turks have had little or no access to any information that might challenge or complicate the official line. The break with the past was greatly aided by Ataturk's Alphabet Revolution (which moved Turkey from the Arabic to a Latinate script, thereby making it impossible for later generations to read anything published before 1928) and also by the Language Revolution that followed: although reformers did not in the end rid Turkish of all words of Arabic or Persian origin, they did manage to excise almost two-thirds of its vocabulary. Offered a single and unchanging version of the past, Turkey's schoolchildren are to this day encouraged not to dwell on it, and to think instead about the great and prosperous nation that Turkey might one day become if all its patriotic citizens forget their tangled Ottoman roots and work together. But as the Republic travels through its ninth decade, it has found itself under growing pressure to democratise, with many of those most in favour of EU accession arguing that Turkey will only truly prosper if it respects the human rights of all its diverse peoples.

To this end, a loose-knit network of grassroots, legal, and academic groups have been arguing for a new definition of Turkishness. In the place of the word 'Turk', which has racial overtones, they have proposed the word *Türkiyeli*, which, because it means 'person of Turkey', would allow its citizens to express ethnic, cultural and/or religious difference while still asserting their allegiance to the nation. While this remains a controversial proposal, there has in recent years been a real and widespread renewal of interest in the Ottoman past, particularly in the area of family history. But even the most superficial investigation, motivated by nothing more than a simple desire to honour one's ancestors, can lead quickly into areas marked taboo.

There are, by some estimates, as many as two million Turks who have at least one grandparent of Armenian extraction. Fethiye Çetin is one of them. She was born in the south-eastern province of Elazığ, in the town of Maden, which straddles the shores of the Tigris River. In Ottoman times Elazığ was one of the empire's six Armenian provinces; today it is home to Azeri and Kurdish as well as ethnic Turks. Fethiye's father worked as a manager at the town's copper works; after his early death, she moved with her mother and siblings into the home of her maternal grandparents. It was only many years later, when she was a law student in Ankara, that her beloved grandmother revealed to her that her real name was not Seher but Heranuş, that she was Armenian by birth, and that she had been plucked from the death march (grabbed from her mother's arms) by the Turkish gendarme who had gone on to raise her as a Muslim. Her story contradicted everything Fethiye knew about her family, her history, and her country. She had assumed herself to be a Muslim Turk; she now discovered a second legacy that threatened to unravel her received identity forever.

Her great achievement in this memoir, written after more than two decades of reflection, is to have cut right through the bitter politics of genocide recognition and denial to tell the human story: to bear witness. Her aim was to 'reconcile us with our history; but also to reconcile us with ourselves'. She wanted to bear witness, to honour, to grieve for all those who lost their lives, their families, and their homes, and to make common cause with all those who wish to make sure that those 'dark days' never return. She wrote it first and foremost for Turkish readers, challenging the distortions of the official history that they all learned as children, and appealing to their common humanity. In this she was far more successful than she could have dreamed. From the day of publication she received, and still receives, numerous calls from people with similar stories, and also from people who simply express their grief. Since its first publication in Turkey in 2004 it has been reprinted seven times. It has also been translated into French, Italian, Eastern and Western Armenian and will soon be available in other languages, including Greek.

Heranuş' mother survived the death march and went on to join her husband in New York, where they started a new family. When Heranuş sat down with her grand-daughter to tell her the truth, her dream was to find the American sister she had never met. She died before that dream could be realised. It was only after Fethiye published her grandmother's death notice in the Istanbul-based Turkish-Armenian weekly, Agos, that a reunion became possible.

The editor of *Agos* was Hrant Dink, who, like Heranuş, dreamed of a day when Turks and Armenians, having faced and mourned their history together, might become good neighbours. When he was prosecuted for insulting Turkishness, Fethiye Çetin acted as his lawyer. On 19 January 2007, after receiving hundreds of death threats but no police protection, Hrant Dink was gunned down outside his office by a young ultranationalist. His murder provoked horror and grief at levels that took the country and indeed the world by surprise. More than 100,000 people turned out for his funeral. Since his death, and despite continuing intimidation, *Agos* has refused to shut down.

Though it retains its Turkish-Armenian focus, it has come to represent all those in Turkey who wish to see an end to unchecked militarism and the ultranationalism that sustains it, and in its place, a democratic society in which diversity is respected and free expression championed. Fethiye Çetin has continued to represent the family, who are still being prosecuted. A member of the Istanbul Bar Association and the Committee to Promote Human Rights, and formerly a spokesperson for the Minority Rights Working Group, she is one of the democracy movement's most courageous advocates. Despite the dangers it faces from what she has called 'obscure forces', she remains confident that democratisation, though slow, jagged and dangerous, cannot be checked. In life, as in this book, her first aim is to give voice to those whom history has silenced. It has been an honour to translate her.

Whenever I think of that January, I shudder; I feel cold. Somewhere deep inside, I begin to ache. When my mother wanted us to know that she was in great pain, she would put her hand on her left breast and say, 'I ache here, just around here.' Somewhere deep inside my heart, I ache in just the same way.

The high walls that enclose the cold mosque courtyard are made from massive stones that are blackened with age but undiminished; the icy funeral stone chills a person just to look at it, and there, on top of it, is a coffin. The slab and its pedestal have both been chiselled from the same great stone. The pedestal is so cold that when I touch it, I fear my hand will stick, so I draw back. It is as if this courtyard – these colossal stones, these giant walls – existed for no other purpose than to make a person feel helpless and bereft.

Whenever I see a funeral stone now, I shudder, no matter what the season, and usually I leave that place at once. But if I linger, it all rushes back – the mosque courtyard, the funeral stone, the freezing cold. And I begin to shiver.

It is night when Emrah rings. 'We've lost our grandmother,' he says. I already know she's dead. In the morning, in the cemetery, in the place where they do the ritual cleansing (they call it a bath house, and so now these words, too, send a chill through me) the women wash down her body and when their work is done, they summon me so that we can say our farewells. I say goodbye to her cold body; I kiss her on the cheeks. On my lips I feel the chill that even now seems so ill-suited to her. I know she's been placed in a coffin but I just can't accept it. It feels like a dream. I cannot believe that my grandmother can be lying so still and helpless, inside that coffin. And neither can I believe how hopelessly the rest of us are going through the motions.

We wait with the women who are huddled together in the most sheltered corner of the mosque courtyard. As we wait, crying uncontrollably as we embrace each new arrival, someone rushes over to us from the huddle of men and in a panic-stricken voice, he asks:

'Auntie Seher's mother and father – what were their names?'

At first none of the women answer. Instead they exchange glances, as the silence becomes ever more awkward. And still the silence goes on, until one of the women, my Aunt Zehra, finally breaks it:

'Her father's name was Hüseyin, and her mother's name was Esma.'

No sooner has my aunt said these words than she turns to me, as if to seek my approval, or so it seems to me.

Relieved to have extracted the answer he wants from this group of tight-lipped women, the man turns back to the all-male crowd that has gathered around the funeral stone, and as he does so, these words rip from my heart through the silence:

'But that's not true! Her mother's name wasn't Esma, it was İsguhı! And her father wasn't Hüseyin, but Hovannes!'

This man has taken it upon himself to furnish the imam with the names of the deceased's parents, and now, just as he prepares to do so, I am declaring those names to be false; he turns around, fixing me with a hostile stare as he struggles to understand what I have said.

My aunts begin to cry. Then all the other women join in, as if my aunts have given them a sign. Usually crying is contagious. I can't stop my tears either. I fall silent, anxious that I might make those around me cry even more if I repeat my accusation or stand by my words. I bow my head as I cry inside, ashamed that even here we have to carry on pretending.

The man stares at the huddle of weeping women for a while longer, and then he gives us a look, as if to say, 'Women!' as he walks away from us.

For the same reason that her mother's name wasn't Esma, and her father's wasn't Hüseyin, my grandmother's real name was not Seher, but Heranuş. This, too, I found out very late.

At the time of Heranuş's childhood, Habab[1] was a large village of 204 dwellings, situated within the boundaries of Palu and the district of Ergani-Maden. The village boasted two churches and one monastery.

Heranuş was the second child to be born to İsguhı and Hovannes[2] Gadaryan. Because she was born after the death of their first child, Markrit, Heranuş was raised with great care. Two more children arrived soon after her. When she was still a tiny girl, Heranuş helped look after these two boys, whose names were Horen and Hırayr.

Heranuş's father Hovannes was the third of seven children and one of six boys. His two older brothers were named Boğos and Stepan, his younger brothers were named Hrant, Garabed, and Manuk, and his only sister was named Zaruhi. The family became bigger still after the eldest brothers married. At an early age, Manuk was afflicted by an unknown malady from whose clutches he was unable to wrest himself free. The entire village went to

1 Though commonly known as Habab, its correct Armenian name was Havav. Today its name is Ekinozu and it belongs to the Kovancilar District.
2 This name appears in the gospels as Hovhannes. In Anatolia alone, there are several variations, such as Ovanes, Ovanis, and Ohannes.

church to pray for his recovery but to no avail. Yet just as the last hope was dying away, Manuk returned to life. The entire village celebrated, for the Gadaryans were its most important family.

Heranuş's grandfather, Hayrabed Efendi, was a highly respected teacher who was known and loved throughout Palu and its environs, as well as Ergani-Maden, and Kiği. He was known as a good man; people listened to what he said. In those days there were colleges in Ergani-Maden and Kiği to which children went to study after finishing primary school. Hayrabed Efendi taught in these colleges. He was a trustee of the church and served as its choirmaster. It was said that his brother, Antreas Gadaryan, was a distinguished teacher who was even better known than he. If people had trouble reading old Armenian texts, they would take them to him. No matter how difficult it was, Antreas would decipher it in no time. In his book entitled *Palu and its Traditions: its education and its intellectual life*,[3] Father Harutyun Sarkisyan wrote these words about him: 'The educator Antreas Gadaryan was a child of Anatolia . . . he was short and spoke very little, but under his thick eyebrows, his bright eyes shone with an intelligence that impressed all those who met him from the moment they made his acquaintance.'

The Gadaryan and Arzumanyan families both had roots in this crowded, long-established village. The Gadaryans' Hovannes was fond of their neighbours' eldest daughter, who was an Arzumanyan , and who, like his own mother, was named İsguhı; a day arrived when his father asked him whether or not he wished to marry their neighbour's daughter. He said 'yes' without hesitation; he was so happy he could almost fly. İsguhı, who was six years younger than him, also came from a big family. She was the eldest, with two younger brothers, and four younger sisters. After Hayk and Sirpuhi came the twin girls, Zaruhi and Diruhi. The youngest was Siranuş.

3 In Armenian, published in Cairo in 1932.

İsguhı's mother Takuhi was the village healer. It was said that she had as much knowledge as a doctor and was sought after throughout the area when there was a case of broken bones. The two families were on the best of terms, so everyone was in favour of Hovannes marrying İsguhı. So it was a love-match, and Heranuş was their second-born. Her godfather was Levon Eliyan, whose own forefathers had been godfathers to many other Gadaryans over the years.

Heranuş was a child who learned fast, and she also had an ear for music. Because she loved to sing, her repertoire was always growing, and she would also try to teach whatever she learned to her sisters, brothers, and cousins. But there was one song she loved more than any other, and she would return to it as often as she could. And when her grandfather sat her on his lap to teach her new songs, he would stroke her hair to let her know how much he liked the way she sang them. She was usually the one to start games; she was the leader, the one who showed the way, and the other children were happy to go along with her.

In 1913, the year Heranuş started school, her father and two of her uncles went to America, in the hope of working to save enough money to set themselves up in business, as a number of their relatives had already done. In those days, many men in the village dreamed of going to America, to work amongst the rich and become wealthy themselves. The first to go to America was Uncle Boğos. Uncle Stepan followed. The next to undertake the long and tumultuous journey were her father and Uncle Hrant.

Heranuş started school the same year as her Uncle Stepan's daughter Maryam, and as soon as she had learned how to read and write, she wrote a letter to her father and her uncles. Maryam wrote her own message on the other side of the same sheet of paper, which they sent to America.

These are the lines that Heranuş wrote on her side of the paper:

Dear Father, Dear Uncles,

We too hope to use our feeble pens to jot down a few lines and tell you how we are, because we know this will please you.

We hope you are well, we all keep hoping and praying that you are well. And we are going to school every day, and we are trying very hard to be well-behaved children.

I kiss your hands, and so do Horen, Hırayr, Jiyayr, and Maryam. Anna misses you very much and she sends you kisses.

Heranuş Gadaryan

The Jirayr she mentions in the letter was, like Maryam, her uncle Stepan's child. Anna was her mother İsguhı's name within the family. On the other side of the paper, Maryam wrote:

Dear Father, Respected Uncle,

I want to jot down a few lines and tell you how we are, because maybe this will please you.

We pray for you to be well, so that we can be well too. Dear and respected fathers, be sure that we never shy away from school, and we are working hard.

Do not worry. But we ask you to please keep writing us letters. We wish that our big Ohan Ahpar and Hrant Ahpar[4] would write us letters, but they don't.

I kiss your hands. Horen, Hırayr, Jirayr, Nektar, and Anna also send their greetings.

Maryam Gadaryan

And so it was that the cousins Heranuş and Maryam sent their good news to their fathers and uncles on two sides of the same sheet of paper. But the beautiful handwriting on one side of the sheet is immediately noticeable. Its words look like flawless pearls; they come from the hand of Heranuş.

---

4 Armenian for 'Big Brother'.

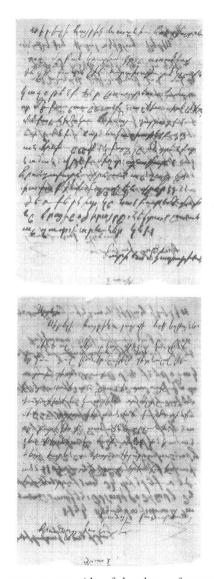

Heranuş wrote on one side of the sheet of paper, and her cousin Maryam on the other. The letter was found in Hovannes' wallet after his death. See p. 8 for translation.

Hovannes and İsguhı loved to dance, and if there was a celebration in the village, they would be there; they would become one with the rhythm of the music and dance the *halay* for hours on end. When her husband went to America, İsguhı would attend weddings and other village festivities with her uncle, to dance the *halay* with him.

In the winter, when the nights were long, the dervishes would come to visit, and that was when the village celebrated most boisterously. The villagers would form a circle around the dervishes, to watch with fear, surprise and adulation as they performed with their skewers and burning braziers. They would send their iron skewers in through one cheek and out the other, but without spilling a single drop of blood. They would take the burning braziers into their arms but their arms and their hands would not burn. Heranuş found the whole business shocking. One day, while she was at school, her brother Horen was scalded by boiling water, and there were terrible burns on the left half of his chest and on his left arm. When Heranuş looked at the burns on her brother's body, she had trouble believing what she'd seen the dervishes do, and would spend long hours at night trying to make sense of it.

The Gadaryans lived in a spacious two-storey house with many rooms and a spacious courtyard. Heranuş was good friends with the dog that guarded the house and enjoyed playing with him. Years later she would tell, over and over, the same wistful stories about this courtyard and the games she played in it with her cousins and the dog. Because most of the men in the family were teachers, and the rest had gone to America, they employed seasonal workers to tend the fields and the crops; these workers and the two domestic servants stayed in rooms that opened onto the courtyard. The family spent its winters in the house in the village, and in the summer moved up to the mountain pastures.

There were a number of looms in the Gadaryan house. Like so many other families in the village, they used them to make *kilims* and multicoloured tablecloths. Heranuş would later remember with affection how her grandfather, who moved to the village after he retired, would sit before the loom trying out new designs, and how he would read the Gospels every evening.

The Gadaryans were a contented and generous family, and their guests were never left wanting. People with unsolved problems came in ever greater numbers to seek out Hayrabed Efendi's expertise. In this crowded and colourful multitude the clever, mature and responsible Heranuş stood out, winning much admiration; no doubt this was partly because she was a beautiful, fair-skinned girl with thick blonde hair. Judging by all these stories, Heranuş was a happy child. In later life, when she talked about her childhood, she would say so herself.

I was born in Ergani-Maden, where Hayrabed Efendi, Heranuş's grandfather, once worked as a teacher. Today it is known simply as Maden, a township in the district of Elazığ. Maden was an old settlement, which sat on two mountain slopes divided by a river valley. The houses looked as if they had been built on top of one another. In the past, Maden had served as a staging post along the Silk Route; the river running through it is the Tigris. An ancient bridge over the Tigris connected the two mountains and the two sides of the city. Whenever it rained heavily, the river waters would rise, sometimes so high as to come right over the bridge. On the bridge were some meagre little shops that looked as if they would collapse unless they huddled together. When the Tigris flooded, the shops would fill with water and the bolts of cloth would float off their shelves along with everything else, bouncing up and down in the river currents until they vanished. Since it was very dangerous to cross the bridge on days when the river was in flood, policemen would be stationed at either end to keep people from doing so. Until the waters had subsided, it was impossible to cross from one side of the city to the other.

My mother and father were married for seven years; when my father died, my mother was twenty-four years old, and she returned to her father's house with three children, one still in swaddling clothes.

Like so many others living in Maden, my father had worked in the Etibank Copper Works. The living quarters for managers and technicians were some way outside the city centre, and it was in one of these dwellings that we lived. But my grandparents' home was an old two-storey house in the market, right in the town centre. The ceilings were very high, as were the capacious window recesses. I took ownership of one of the windows that looked out onto the market. The base and the top of the window were made of wood, and the recess was so large that I could play here, and do drawings; I could watch Aunt Sabahat and Uncle Mesut (who was only three years older than me) do their writing, and in the same place I would sing songs and recite the poems I had learned by heart. Whenever I did so, this window was my stage. If there was anyone to listen, I would give concerts that I never knew how to end.

It wasn't just the windows I loved, but the whole house and everyone in it, so much so that whenever we went to visit my grandmother, and I realised that it was almost time to go home, I would play tricks to keep us from leaving. My father never fell for these ruses but sometimes when my grandmother kept insisting ('Let her stay with us!') he would say, 'All right, let her stay,' and with these words, the world became mine. But I didn't always get my way. Once, when I was too stubborn to yield, even though I knew the game was up, my father carried me all the way home in his arms.

My Aunt Sabahat and my Uncle Mesut went to school. To be surrounded by their bags, notebooks, pens, and coloured pencils, to watch them wink at each other as they and their friends pretended to include me in their games, – these pleasures were reason enough for me to employ any number of childish tricks to stay in that house.

Saddled as she was with three small children, my mother had a short fuse, so I looked forward to going to my grandparents' house, where they and Aunt Zehra were patient with us and full of compassion. This must be why, even at the age of two, I would pack a few random things under my arm (a single sock, a knitting needle, a dustcloth) and, every time I found an open door, would seize my chance to head straight for my grandmother's house. But every time I'd be picked up by someone who knew us and taken home.

One night, my mother, my sister, my brother and I stayed over at my grandparents' house. Haluk was newborn and in swaddling clothes. Handan was still in nappies and had a pacifier in her mouth. My father had dropped us off at my grandparents' on his way to Diyarbakır.

According to what I found out later, there had been a phone call from Diyarbakır – 'The item you ordered has arrived' – and my father had gone off to collect it. Apparently, it was a Singer sewing machine with pedals. He'd been planning to return with it the next day.

That night, we played cards until very late. My grandmother's favourite game was 'elevens', and she played it well. She taught it to me, too. Or at least I thought I'd learned. I would so enjoy watching them play, and from time to time I'd say a silent prayer in the hope that they might include me in the game.

The next morning, there was a rapid, noisy knocking on the door. To hear a knock on that door was such an unusual thing that everyone in the house panicked and came clattering down the wooden stairs. I stopped at the top of the stairs so that I could see what was going on below. The man at the door, who was out of breath, was calling my grandfather to the post office. 'Uncle Fikri, they're calling you from Diyarbakır. You must come to the post office straight away.'

As my grandfather put on his shoes and his coat, the other members of the household rushed around trying to help him. 'Don't panic,' he said, 'just hope for the best, be patient,' but he himself couldn't find one of his shoes, and then he was putting it on the wrong foot. Finally he left and headed for the post office.

After he was gone, a nervous, fearful silence set in as we sat and waited. I could see the post office from my window. Sensing that things were happening that I should not miss, I went upstairs to sit at my window. I glued my eyes to the post office.

Some time later, two men holding my grandfather's arms carried him out of the building. He couldn't walk, he looked utterly shattered. As he drew closer, I could see he'd been crying.

Inside the house, the screams mixed with tears and the sound of running feet. My mother and my aunt were crying so hard they nearly threw themselves down the wooden stairs. They were screaming. My father was dead. He'd had a heart attack; he'd failed to rally. This is what they'd said on the phone.

After my father's death, we moved to my grandparents' house – my mother, my sister, my brother, and me. So we were all together, all the time. But I missed my father. One day I secretly followed my mother and the others to the cemetery, and though I discovered there that my father was buried under the ground, I still waited, still hoped, for his return. I waited for years. The concerts in the window sill came to an end, but my memory of grandfather coming out of the post office held by two men, and of the panic-stricken footsteps on the wooden stairs – these were engraved in my mind, and for years they haunted me.

We left the company house and, together with my grandparents, moved to a larger house that was close to the school. When he had graduated from the veterinary faculty in Ankara, my Uncle Mahmut came back to live with us for a while before doing his military service.

Uncle Mahmut, the eldest of five children, tried to comfort my mother, telling her that 'the responsibility for you and the three children rests on my shoulders, so please don't worry'. Because my grandfather's wages only just covered his own family's household expenses. There were already five people living there, and with the four of us, that made nine. A little later, we moved to the Mahmudiye stud farm to stay with my uncle Mahmut, who trained colts. When my uncle married, it was decided that the time had come for us to 'climb off his shoulders' and we returned to my grandparents.

There might not have been enough money to make ends meet, but there were two things in this house that were never lacking. The first was love, and the second was food. This was a family that liked good food; they were willing to cut back on anything else in order to be able to eat well.

My grandfather was a cheerful, charming, well-meaning man – unless he was hungry, and then he was impossible. Once he'd eaten his fill, he'd return to his old gentle, affable self, and it was as if that fractious, belligerent man we'd just seen had never existed. When he was going through one of his hunger crises, my grandmother would go into overdrive, rushing to get him his food while imploring him to act sensibly, reasonably, and all the while trying to protect the rest of us from his wrath. At times like these, we'd creep away to wait for him to eat his fill.

My grandfather was a shift worker at the factory, and he usually worked nights; during Ramadan, the month of fasting, it was the shift he preferred. Everyone in the house was emphatically in favour of his taking the special Ramadan night shift, as was most of the neighbourhood, and we would all pray that nothing would happen to take him off it until the month had ended. Because if he was on the night shift, he could sleep all day and fast while he slept.

Whatever shift he was on, no one but my grandmother dared to go near him on days when he fasted, not until the sun had set and we could sit down to eat.

My grandfather would not be woken up until just before the *iftar*[5] and that was how he was spared his hunger pangs and we the wrath of a grandfather whose eyes would roll to the back of his head when his stomach was empty. When he had washed his face and come to the table, we children had the job of telling him that

5 The hours between sunset and sunrise, when one is allowed to break one's fast during Ramadan.

the call to prayer was underway or that the cannon had sounded. He would sit down, fill his spoon with soup, raise it to his lips and wait for us to say, 'Grandad, the call to prayer is over!', but if the wait went on too long, he would get angry at the *hoca* and shout out, 'Sing the call to prayer, father – hey father! – read it now!' and if still nothing happened, would begin to rail against him. He'd fling the spoon down, spring up and shake his fist, and would then sit down again, fill his spoon with soup and resume the same position as before: 'God give me patience, father! Hey father, can you sing it now?'

One evening, my grandfather came home to find guests in the house. We could tell he was hungry from the colour of his face and also from the way he walked. So famished was he that his face darkened the moment he entered the house; he walked towards the women visitors with a heavy, ominous tread. The women all jumped to their feet as a sign of respect. They waited for my grandfather to say, 'How good to see you, please sit down, make yourselves comfortable,' but instead he fixed my grandmother with a stare as he breathed heavily through his nose; the women were left standing. My grandfather went over to my grandmother and hissed into her ear loud enough for the guests to hear:

'Don't these women have children or families? What are they doing away from their houses at this hour, why won't they go home?' My grandmother glared at him angrily:

'Oi, Müsürman,[6] she whispered.

As the women watched, still standing, they broke into smiles, showing no sign of anger or offence.

'It's time for us to go, anyway. Uncle Fikri's hungry,' they said, and with that they left. In those days, everyone called my grandfather 'Uncle Fikri'; later, he became everyone's 'grand-father'. No one got upset about the things he said – not then, not ever – and no one took offence.

6 A colloquial Turkish term for 'Muslim'.

Early 1965. From left to right: my brother Haluk, Aunt
Sabahat, me, my mother, my sister Handan, my grandmother
and grandfather. He was in one of his worst moods that day.

Whenever my grandmother got angry at my grandfather, she would say 'Oi, Müsürman!' She put the stress on the first syllable of Muslim, making her anger and vitriol clear. At times like this, my grandfather would say 'Oi, Hürme!' and he, too, would put the stress on the first syllable.

Whenever we heard them use the word 'Oi' with each other, we'd try to make ourselves scarce – to wait for the storm to pass and for our grandfather to fill his stomach.

But my mother, who was a keen observer and an excellent mimic, would follow these arguments closely and later, when the house was once more peaceful and quiet, she would amuse us by wittily repeating all that had been said, imitating both my grandparents. We'd fall about laughing.

My grandfather, who would have eaten by then, and who would have returned to his usual charming self, would enjoy these skits as much as the rest of us, and would often take part in them. But my grandmother would shake her head and say, 'We've turned into a family of buffoons,' casting furious, reproachful looks in my grandfather's direction. Seeing the anger in her eyes, my grandfather would try to placate her. 'Oi, woman! Why so angry, didn't I give you the three most beautiful daughters in the world? What else could you possibly want?' he would say, and would gaze with love and pride at the three daughters whose beauty he had just praised.

My grandmother always protected us. When my mother was angry with us, she'd threaten us with her slipper. When she saw this, my grandmother would stand in front of my mother and stop her, calming her down, and we, always knowing the best escape, rushed to take refuge in our grandmother's arms.

Children often test the limits of their elders, and there must have been moments when we tried our grandmother's patience, too. But she was always patient and compassionate with us. I cannot remember a single time when she vented anger on us or

1957. From left to right: Aunt Sabahat,
Aunt Zehra and my mother, Vehbiye.

said a harsh word. But she was sometimes strict with her other grandchildren, and at times scolded them. For her, though, we were charges who were to be protected at all times – fragile children to be treated with the utmost care.

Throughout her life, that was how she treated us. This preferential treatment sometimes provoked some jealousy in other parts of the family; sometimes we were sarcastically referred to as the 'precious grandchildren'.

I was told that I resembled my father, and that my sister Handan took after my mother, who was a beautiful woman. When people met us for the first time, they'd say: 'Fethiye looks like her father, and Handan her mother.' I knew exactly what these words meant: Handan was beautiful and I was ugly. My grandmother would get upset when people said this – as they did all the time. She would take me on her lap, stroke my hair, and declare in a loud, stern voice, 'All my girl needs are her eyes!' Once she was sure she had everyone's attention, she would intone, 'It's the eyes and the eyebrows that count, the rest is mere words!' Having recited that old proverb, she would look lovingly into my eyes. There was something so haughty in her voice, so righteous and didactic, that nothing more would be said on the matter, apart from a few polite comments about my eyes and eyebrows.

My grandfather, who did not get much pleasure from work, retired as soon as he had worked the requisite time. In the early days of his retirement, before he ran through his lump sum, he kept insisting that he was going on a pilgrimage to Mecca. But my grandmother never once gave him her approval for this plan. Every time he brought up the pilgrimage, she would say, 'Oi, Müsürman, the pilgrimage is to your own door,' and as she spoke she would give us a signal with her eyes. In the end my grandfather was unable to go to Mecca; his lump sum went on food, and was soon exhausted.

His greatest pleasure in life was food. His favourite dishes were elaborate stews with lots of meat, butter, and tomato sauce; he usually had to hire a porter to carry the meat home from the butcher. His medium of exchange wasn't money but meat. He'd measure the prices of all things against meat. If he had just bought a pullover, he would work out how many kilos of meat he could have bought with the same sum and usually it made him unhappy to think of all the meat he had foregone.

'How much did you pay for this shirt?' After working out the quantity of meat he could have bought for the price of the shirt, he'd say, 'Imagine, spending all that on clothes.' And he would add with a moan, 'It's such a shame, isn't it, when you think that we could have bought x kilos of meat with that money.' Or he'd reproach us like this: 'Instead of spending all that money on shoes, wouldn't it have been better if we'd bought five kilos of meat?'

When guests came to visit from other provinces or districts, his first question after everyone had exchanged the usual greetings was, 'What's the price of meat there?' It angered him when people replied, 'I don't know', as he couldn't understand how it was possible not to know the answer: 'Now how could someone not know the price of meat in the place where they lived!'

Wherever we went, we had to find out the price of meat, knowing full well what the question would be when we returned.

So wherever we were, we had to find out how much meat cost, and if we ever forgot, we did not dare leave the question unanswered; instead we made something up to placate him. We lied, we fooled him.

Though he'd been treated badly, and had often been fooled, my grandfather never lost his faith in people; certain merchants assumed from this that he must be a bit simple-minded, and it was not uncommon for them to talk him into buying spoiled goods – for example, a huge joint that had begun to smell. When the bad meat reached the house, there would be another harsh exchange in which the word 'oi' featured a great deal, and though it would end with my grandfather admitting that he had been cheated, he would never offer to take the meat back. This matter (like so many others) was left to my grandmother to resolve: in a huff, she would pick up the offending parcel and leave for the market.

There, she would find the merchant, give him a good scolding for what he had done and return the spoiled goods. When neighbours saw my grandmother racing in the direction of the market with her bag in hand, or something under her arm, they would twitter and ask my mother, 'What did Uncle Fikri buy this time?' My mother and other young women of the neighbourhood would add this latest episode to their repertoire of stories and imitations to be enjoyed in the evening.

One day my grandfather came home from the market with a large basket of grapes. After taking a good long look at them, my grandmother pronounced, 'These grapes have no life left in them, they're no longer edible. Take them back to where they came from!' As usual, my grandfather refused at first to admit the grapes were spoiled. To show my grandmother how unfair she was being, and to prove how beautiful the grapes really were, he picked up a bunch – but as he raised his hand all the grapes fell into the basket, leaving him clutching only the stem. As usual, the rest of us were watching from a distance, gripped with silent laughter.

My grandfather searched the basket for a bunch of grapes that were still on their stem, and when he found one he showed it to my grandmother, and then to the rest of us, saying 'Grace be to God, look at these grapes!' But the next bunch he selected didn't look at all like the previous one; he picked it up hopefully but was again left holding only the stem. Quickly putting it to one side, he fell to searching the basket once again.

After peering into the depths of the basket my grandfather was forced, in the end, to admit that the grapes were off. His performance was over; as always, he gave up, fell into a deep silence, and for a long time would keep a low profile in the neighbourhood. He left it to my grandmother to bring the matter to a close: picking up the basket, she headed off to the market.

My grandmother was quick-witted and resourceful, and so good at solving problems – not just in the market, but in many other areas of life – that sometimes, in such situations, my grandfather sometimes gave her the admiring nickname 'Sergeant Seher'. To describe her industry and dynamism, my mother called her 'Mistress Storm'.

There seemed to be nothing she couldn't do. If she wasn't rolling my grandfather's cigarettes, or putting them in the silver tobacco box, or 'cupping' with hot jars on his back whenever he had a cold, or pouring molten lead into cold water over the head of someone who thought themselves to have been cursed by the evil eye, she was gathering up old pieces of cloth and sewing them together to make patterned and colour-coordinated tablecloths and prayer rugs, or knitting socks and gloves with five knitting needles.

My grandmother was also famous for her cooking. No matter how difficult and elaborate a dish was, in her hands, it was full of flavour, and anyone who ate it could not stop talking about it. She made beautiful bulgur-wheat balls stuffed with walnuts, raisins, meat and onions, and *kaburga dolma, maden köfte, hilorik şkisi, şkili dolma, kibe mumbar, kibe kuduru,* and *meftune*[7], and no one could stop talking about how tasty they were: 'To go over to the other side without having eaten her *kibe mumbar* would be unthinkable.' People would say that she had 'passed her gift to her daughters' – their way of saying that my mother's and aunts' cooking was just as flavourful as my grandmother's.

This was how my grandmother explained the 'secret' behind her cooking: 'To bring out the full flavour, you should never skimp on ingredients. You should use plenty of meat, butter, and tomato sauce. In other words, don't be sparing. And then, when you put it on the flame, don't neglect it. You have to put your whole soul into the food, and while the meal is cooking you have to cook with it too.'

Her daughters, grandchildren, neighbours and friends were always asking for her recipes. We'd often see her giving out their details, and as she recited them, she would speak like a teacher who loved her work. We heard her passing on some recipes so often that we learned them by heart. I can still recite her recipe for *meftune*, a dish much loved in our part of the world. This is how my grandmother told me how to make it:

7 Traditional meat dishes.

'Buy a well-fatted joint of kid goat. Don't take off a single mouthful, and don't chop it up – place the whole thing at the bottom of the saucepan.' As she said this, she'd demonstrate with her hands just how the join should be laid in the saucepan. 'Chop up the aubergines and put them over the meat. Chop up two ripe tomatoes, and two green chilli peppers. Then take the sumac water that you've prepared in advance, and pour it over all the ingredients – and don't skimp on it. After you've brought it to the boil twice over a high flame, turn down the heat. Fifteen minutes before you take the saucepan off the flame, fill up a little cup with water and pour it in, to separate the fat.'

She also placed importance on the way *meftune* was served when it was ready. There was a special sauce to accompany it, made with crushed green peppers and garlic, and you poured it over the dish after it had been served onto plates, which would then be decorated with finely chopped parsley. The *meftune* would then be brought to the table with bulgur and vermicelli.

I don't remember ever being hungry when I was a child. Living as I did in a family that took its food and drink so seriously, food for me was a form of torture. Years later, recognising the taste of a dish I'd refused to eat as a child, I would realise what I'd missed, but during my childhood I hated mealtimes.

My mother would try to force me to eat; mealtimes were battles that would end with my mother shouting and screaming and threatening me with her slipper. I would rush to my grand-mother's side, knowing this to be the best escape route. With the greatest forbearance, my grandmother would bring me tea, bread and cheese – the only three things I would consent to eat. She was very patient and compassionate with us, and to tell the truth, we three children knew our limits, too. Even so, there were times when we longed for something that we could not quite put into words. It would be at times like these that my grandmother would sense what we desired, and she would do everything she could to make us happy, pampering us, taking us on her knee, and stroking us on the back.

As soon as my grandmother sat down, Handan and Haluk would clamber onto her lap and begin to play with her shrivelled breasts. She would wait patiently for them to tire of this game; never once did she push them away.

On days when we were sad, she would tell us the tale of Sister Pizez[8]. She had told this story first to her own children, and then to us; later on, she would tell it to her grandchildren's children.

On cold winter evenings we would trap our grandmother in front of the stove and would clamour for the story of Sister Pizez.

'Please, Granny, tell us the story of Sister Pizez. What is Sister Pizez, Granny?'

'Sister Pizez is a winged beetle,' she would say.

And she would begin to tell her story.

Sister Pizez had a load of dirty laundry. She was taking it up to wash it in the stream when she ran into a hedgehog. 'Sister Pizez, will you marry me?' asked the hedgehog. This is how Sister Pizez replied:

'When you're angry, will you beat me?' she asked the hedgehog.

'I certainly will,' said the hedgehog.

'All right then, so tell me what you'd use to beat me,' said Sister Pizez. 'I'll sink my bristles into you,' said the hedgehog. When she heard that, Sister Pizez turned down the hedgehog's marriage proposal and continued on her way to the stream.

Before long, she ran into a cat. The cat, too, made a marriage proposal. Sister Pizez asked him the same question she had asked the hedgehog. 'When you're angry, what will you beat me with?' 'If you make me angry,' said the cat, 'I'll scratch you.' Upon hearing his answer, Sister Pizez rejected his offer of marriage and continued on her way to the stream.

8 *Pizez* is the Armenian word for flies with sheathlike wings.

Before long, she ran into Mister Rat. Mister Rat asked Sister Pizez the same question. 'Mistress Pizez, will you marry me?' And Sister Pizez asked Mister Rat, 'When you're angry, what will you beat me with?' Mister Rat showed her his tail and said, 'With this sweet little tail of mine.' Looking at the tail, she thought to herself, 'This rat's tail is soft, it won't hurt.' She accepted Mister Rat's proposal and they walked on to the stream together to wash the clothes.

Before long, they heard music coming from the Bey's house in the distance. Knowing that there was a wedding at the Bey's house, and knowing that they would be inviting the guests to a feast, Mister Rat said, 'Let me run off now to the Bey's house and bring back some food. We're hungry, after all. After we've filled our stomachs, we can finish the laundry.' With that, he left the riverside, and rushed off to find some food to bring back.

But when he got to the house, Mister Rat was so taken with the cauldrons full of food, and the music, and the fun, that he forgot all about Sister Pizez. He just ate and danced and enjoyed himself.

Meanwhile, Sister Pizez washed her laundry and beat it against the stones, and then, leaning over the stream to scoop out a cup of water, fell into the water and couldn't save herself. Just then a party making its way to the Bey's house on horseback stopped by the stream to water the horses. While they were drinking their water, the horses heard a voice coming to them from the depths. This is what Sister Pizez cried out:

'Horsemen, oh horsemen, you sweet creatures with your pockets full,
When you get to the Bey's house,
And you see Mister Rat,
Tell me that Sister Pizez has fallen into the stream, and tell him
to come at once!

The horsemen heard the voice, but they could see no one. They couldn't figure out where the voice was coming from. Before long, they were forced to continue their journey to the Bey's house. As soon as they got there, they told everyone about the voice they'd heard by the side of the stream.

Mister Rat also heard what they said. Remembering his forgotten wife, he left the Bey's house and raced back to the stream. Finding Sister Pizez by the side of the stream, he said:

'Give me your hand so I can helpahelp you.'

Because Sister Pizez was very angry at Mister Rat, she replied:

'Not until I tell you how crossaloss I am.'

'Give me your hand so I can helpahelp you'

'Not until I tell you how crossaloss I am. You've been off gallivanting for three days, ho ho ho, and I am very cross with you, ho ho.'

'Be cross, then, ho ho, and be done with you,' said Mister Rat, and picking up a handful of mud, he threw it at Sister Pizez and ran off.

My grandmother's children, grandchildren, and great-grandchildren all grew up hearing this story, and they all went on to tell it to their own children. What we liked most, I think, were the repetitions of nonsense words at the end: 'Give me your hand so I can helpahelp you.' 'Not until I tell you how crossaloss I am . . .'

After my father died, there were no more toys for me, nor did I have a hankering for any. But, even though I never said so, I did long for a musical instrument. When the other children were busy playing house, I would find a piece of wood, stretch wires across it, and try to get different sounds out of them. Sometimes I would stretch rubber bands of different thicknesses alongside the wires, ordering them according to the tension.

Then one day my Uncle Mahmut gave my little uncle, Mesut, a mandolin. Uncle Mesut was at a boarding school in Diyarbakır and he took his mandolin back with him. I could hardly wait for him to come home for the holidays. But even more, because he'd come home with his mandolin.

Uncle Mesut had learned the old Turkish folksong, 'The train comes, and it is welcome' and when he came home he would play it for us. After watching him closely, I took the mandolin and begin to play the song I'd just heard.

I don't know how it was that I could play the mandolin the moment I picked it up, but when the other people in our house saw that I could, it was decided that the mandolin should be left with me. From then on, I played it whenever I could, and though I could not read music, I managed to work out how to play every song I heard.

When Handan sang with her beautiful voice, Haluk would keep time on an overturned 'Vita Oil' tin and I would accompany them on the mandolin. During the day we would practice the songs people liked, and in the evenings would give concerts. All of us – mother, aunts, my sister and brother – loved to sing. My mother and my aunts were known for their lovely voices. I would play and they would sing. Nearly everyone would join in – but never once did I hear my grandmother singing. She'd never join in with any Turkish folksong, though every once in a while, if it was a tune she liked, she would keep the tempo with her hand.

She was proud that I had an aptitude for music, and when she praised me, would say, 'You take after our side of the family.' I did not do too badly at school either. When she saw the reports I brought home from school, she would be very pleased, 'After all, you and Uncle Mahmut take after our side of the family.' At the time I had no idea what she was saying beyond the fact that she was paying me a compliment: it would be years before I understood what she really meant.

Twice a year my mother would empty her trunk, pass her hands over everything it contained, and pack it up again with the painstaking care of an artist. We loved these days when she aired her trunk. We'd sit beside her, examining each object as our mother took it out. It contained mostly tablecloths, embroideries and lacework that my mother had made for her trousseau, along with the perfumes, pieces of jewellery and little presents our father had bought for her.

Our favourites were a purplish-brown satin dressing gown, the likes of which we had only seen in foreign films, and a comb, brush and mirror set that came from the same world. Every time we saw these things, we'd beg our mother to put on the dressing gown and brush her hair while looking into that beautiful mirror.

In fact, she'd be longing to do just that, so she would put on the dressing gown and, looking into the mirror, would brush her hair, throwing it back from time to time like one of those movie stars. It was a scene we adored. It was said that Uncle Mahmut had brought the dressing gown and the mirror and brush set back with him from America. At the time, Uncle Mahmut had been studying in England. The idea that he might have been to America struck us as entirely natural, and it didn't occur to us to ask for the details.

When my grandfather returned from prayer one afternoon, I had my mandolin in my hands, practicing for a concert. As usual, he coughed to let us know that he was coming in.

The reason for his noisy entrance was to give the women and children a chance to hide anything they might have been doing that they did not wish my grandfather to see. For example, my mother smoked in front of everyone except my grandfather. My grandfather knew this, but he acted as if he didn't, and it was to avoid shaming her that he would make such a noisy entrance; he also gave her enough time to put out the cigarette and conceal the evidence.

'Today, in the mosque, the *hoca* gave a sermon about the mandolin,' he said. He waited until he had everyone's attention before. 'He said it was a sin to play the mandolin. The *hoca* told us not to enter into sin by buying our children mandolins; he said that instead of giving them mandolin lessons, we should send them to study the Koran.'

Without missing a beat, my grandmother stepped in. 'Was it the *hoca* who said all this?' she asked, so that she could be sure of the facts.

'Yes, he was the one,' said my grandfather, and my grandmother cried out in anger: 'Blast that *hoca*! What makes playing the mandolin a sin? If he or his children had a gift for the mandolin, he wouldn't be talking like that.'

Then she told my grandfather, 'Don't bring that ignorant *hoca*'s idiotic words back into this house again.' Having taken the matter in hand and silenced my grandfather, she then nodded for me to continue. I felt grateful to my grandmother. But perhaps my grandfather didn't quite believe what he had heard in the mosque either, because after this incident, he never did a thing to stop our concerts with the mandolin and the Vita Oil can.

My grandparents were both good Muslims. But my grandmother had no time for bigotry or lack of reason, and was not afraid to speak out against anyone who spoke unjustly, even if that person was an imam; after admonishing everyone in the room, she would in the end, manage to persuade my grandfather, whom it suited to remain under her influence.

In the morning, we went to the cemetery. My grandmother had been taken from the hospital morgue to the cemetery bath house. Here they would ritually cleanse her before wrapping her in a shroud. So we all headed for the cemetery – her children, her grandchildren, her great-grandchildren, her sons-in-law. Only the women were allowed in while she was being washed; the men would say their farewells to my grandmother after she had been cleansed and shrouded.

The four women attendants inside, hoping to draw attention to their fine work and to show what a big tip they deserved, were praying in loud voices while washing my grandmother with soft and soapy loofahs, after which they would pour hot water over her; each time they repeated this ritual, they would look at us.

My grandmother loved cleanliness. Had she been able to raise her head at that moment, I am sure she would have turned to these women who were washing her with those soapy loofahs and said, 'Don't just caress me with those loofahs – rub me as hard as you can and get all the dirt out.'

My grandmother didn't take to dirty or slovenly people: if ever someone tried to make a connection between uncleanliness and poverty, she would refuse to countenance it, saying, 'Cleanliness is only a cake of soap away, my girl. Dirtiness has nothing to do with being poor.'

After soaping her down a few times with their sponges, the attendants filled a hamam bowl with water and gave it to Aunt Zehra. 'Why don't you each pour some water over her now?', they said, 'It will ease your suffering.' First Aunt Zehra and Aunt Sabahat embraced their mother and cried, and then they each poured water over her in turn. Handan, who had arrived from Ankara, poured water over her first and then, embracing her grandmother, she began to recite 'Sister Clean, Sister Clean' like a dirge, as she cried uncontrollably.

My grandmother was renowned for her cleanliness. The moment anyone walked into her threadbare provincial house, in which there were no modern conveniences, the first thing that hit them was the sweet smell of soap. Some of the houses we lived in had wooden ceilings, floors, and windows. My mother, my grandmother, and my sisters would scrub and scrub those boards with brushes and soapy water until they were sparkling white. Whenever they reproached anyone whose floors and windows were not sparkling white they would be secretly congratulating themselves on theirs.

After they were washed, underwear and scarves made from white cambric would be boiled in a pot for hours on end, and the house would be fragrant with that cleansing boiling smell I can still recall today.

As they proudly hung their whites outside, Seher Hanım and her daughters would listen (without quite appearing to do so) to what neighbours and passers-by had to say about them; but they never hid their pleasure at hearing what people said because our laundry was famous throughout Maden for its whiteness and for the sweet smell it gave out as it dried. People walking past our house would see the bright white laundry flapping in the wind, and those to whom the sight was familiar would always say a few words before continuing on their way.

Laundry days would begin with the *tahfir* ritual. *Tahfir* meant washing certain pieces of laundry with soap under running water before putting them into the tub. The clothes that received this treatment were pyjama bottoms, trousers, underwear and socks. My grandmother's explanation was simple: 'Urine's spilled over these things in the toilet. They can't go into the tub until they've been washed.'

The toilets in Maden were made of stone: there was a hole, and there were two recesses in which to place your feet. 'No matter how careful you are in the toilet, you still can't keep urine getting on you,' she would say. So laundry day would always begin with their taking any piece of clothing that might have come in contact with urine and 'passing it through water' – or in other words, washing it first under running water.

The next job was to remove the elastic from the waists and cuffs of pyjamas and suchlike, for the elastic was to be washed separately. After the whites had been boiled and dried, all the laundry would be ironed, and after the elastic bands had been 'hot-ironed' they would be put back and tied up with a hook needle or a buckle, and then the laundry would be carefully folded and everything put back where it belonged. So did the ritual go on every laundry day.

It angered my grandfather that laundry days were so frequent. 'You wash things so much you're wearing everything out; clothes can't take such punishment,' he'd say; but none of the women in the house took his words too seriously.

The *tahfir* ritual would continue even after we had bought a washing machine and used it for all the laundry. Certain items did not go into the machine unless they had been washed in advance – and if socks, having been passed through water and then washed in the machine, were still not clean enough, they would be washed again by hand.

My grandmother loved to go out on visits and excursions; she loved eating, and eating out; but she was so concerned about cleanliness that if she was ever offered refreshment in a place she found slovenly, she would refuse it, saying, 'Thanks, but I'm fasting.' Whoever had offered her the food or drink would not hesitate to take this honest, candid, falsehood-hating woman at face value; as they drew away, they would say, 'As God wishes.'

When we were alone again, I'd tease her: 'You tell us not to lie, but you lie, too. Isn't lying a sin, grandmother?' She'd look very annoyed, and say, 'You're right, my girl, and may God forgive me, but what could I do? That place was filthy.'

Hamam days I hated, except for the trip home. Divining that our ablutions at home were not enough to get us clean, and refusing to listen to any of our complaints and objections, our grandmother would march us all off to the hamam. The bathgloves and loofahs, the hot water and the steam – they hurt our young skin; to us, the hamam was a form of punishment; it was to get through them as fast as we could that we submitted to these torture sessions without protest. But the trip home from the hamam remains one of my most cherished memories. The moment we stepped into the house, squeaky clean and smelling of soap, the grown-ups would light the stove that they'd readied before our departure, and before long the teakettle standing ready on top of the stove would begin to rattle and boil. We would loll on the cushions behind the stove, stretching like cats.

A few years after my father died, I noticed certain secret discussions going on, aided by winks and nods, and conducted in whispers so that we children could not hear. As you know, adults think they can hide their discussions from children, but in fact children hear everything and pick up on whatever is going on. From the bits and pieces that I overheard, it transpired that a number of men were in love with my mother and wished to marry her.

Sometimes go-betweens would come to the house and shut themselves up in a room with my grandmother; they would then leave looking very mysterious. Whenever these people came, they wouldn't let us into the room, but after they left I would pretend to be playing and paying no attention, while eavesdropping on everything people said.

Once, when they thought we were asleep and so did not speak in low voices, I heard what they were saying very clearly. My grandmother told my mother, 'Look, my girl, you're young, you're beautiful, get married. If there's anyone you love, anyone who suits you, don't shy away, marry him.'

But my mother objected: 'I'm not raising my children with a stepfather.' To which my grandmother retorted, 'Don't worry about the children, I'll look after them. Don't waste your youth.' Later on, I heard her repeat this over and over: 'If you want this, my girl, don't you worry. You get married, and I can look after the children.'

I never found out whether or not my mother had wanted to remarry, but she never did. When I overheard that conversation, the thought that our mother might leave us sent me into a panic; I told no one what I had heard, but spent several sleepless nights worrying about what might happen.

But when I think back to those days, I understand my grandmother's insistence differently. Though they lived in a repressive, conservative provincial town, she was still urging her daughter, a 'widowed woman', to make a free choice, to enjoy a sex life.

There were three cinemas in Maden. The most distant from the house was owned by the factory and known in the town as the 'company cinema': here they would show foreign-language films with subtitles, and only at night. This was why we could only attend the 'company cinema' with an adult. Much though she would have liked to do so, my mother, as a widowed woman, did not dare go to the cinema at night, for fear of gossip. My grandfather was no use either. So it was our grandmother we begged to take us there. She had no desire to go herself – as she was unable to read or write, she couldn't follow the subtitles – so she would drop us off at the company cinema and then go on elsewhere.

The Ozan cinema was right above our house. It had an enclosed theatre for the winter and an open-air theatre for the summer. We saw every film they showed in the summer cinema, and would watch each screening until its run was over, memorising all the lines. The soundtrack was loud enough for us to hear it inside the house

Then there was the Sezer cinema, which was across the Tigris, on the mountainside opposite our house. To get there, we had to walk across the ancient bridge and through the market.

There was an intense rivalry between these two cinemas. They would show two, sometimes three films back to back, and would compete for patronage by sending men out into the streets with megaphones and billboards advertising the films. Women preferred the weepies with Muhterem Nur and Ayşecik.[9] A film was only as good as the number of tears it caused its viewers to shed.

One day, one of the megaphone men shouted out: 'This film will make you weep and weep. It will make you weep so much that you won't need to bring just one handkerchief with you. Bring ten!'

The women who heard him lost all interest in their work and went running to see the film. Seeing how effective the handkerchief ploy had been, and thinking this might be a good way to promote films, the megaphone man from the other cinema went out into the streets the next day crying:

'This film is going to make you cry so much, that handkerchiefs won't be enough! Bring a sheet – not just one sheet, but five!'

They would let us go to daytime performances at the Sezer or the Ozan cinemas even if there wasn't an adult to take us. Our biggest treat was to fill our pockets with the melon and

9 Well-known Turkish actresses of the 1950s and 1960s.

watermelon seeds our grandmother gave us and head for the Saturday matinee. The seeds from the watermelons we ate during the summer were never thrown away; instead they were washed and dried. Then my grandmother would boil them in salted water, pour them onto a metal sheet and roast them over a flame. She'd wash the melon seeds in salted water, too. Whenever we went to the cinema, our pockets were stuffed with these seeds. It was schoolchildren who went to these matinees. As we children munched on our seeds, we would laugh out loud together during the comic scenes, cry together during the sad scenes, shout out during the action scenes to cheer on the leading man – and if we were happy with the ending, we would applaud together.

That day was the first day of the holidays; we had just been given our reports. We three children crossed over to the Sezer cinema in the market. Because it was showing two films back to back that day, we were inside for a long time.

When the film finished, there was an announcement before the lights came on. 'Alo, alo. Attention, attention! (In Maden all announcements began like this.) 'Alo, alo. Attention, attention! Everyone stay in their seats. Sit quietly and wait!' Those who had already stood up sat down again, and we all waited.

A while later, we learned what had happened from the mothers and fathers who came to pick up their children. A rainstorm had flooded the entire town, the river had burst its banks, and the bridges were under water.

The ancient bridge, too, had been closed to all traffic – even to pedestrians – until the following day. The shops on the bridge had been flooded and the bridge itself was in danger. The families who lived on this side of the river would be able to collect their children; the families who lived on the other side of the river would not.

I became anxious and fearful. I was in charge of my younger brother and sister, and had to come up with a solution before they could see I was scared. In the end I decided to look for the cinema owner, Uncle Faik.

Uncle Faik was a close friend of my father and my uncle. He would never leave us stranded in a situation like this; he would definitely work something out. The three of us got up and headed for the cinema door, where we were stopped. I said that we wanted to see Uncle Faik. 'You wait inside,' said the doorman. 'I'll let Uncle Faik know.'

We sat, we waited, but the doorman did not budge from his position, and he didn't pass on our message to Uncle Faik. A while later, when we had again stood up and gone to the door, a woman rushed through the door. It was my grandmother. We ran into her arms. Without making a fuss she hurried us outside as fast as she could.

After passing through the market, we headed for the bridge. Crowds had gathered on both sides of the river. The police were not letting anyone cross, but people were pleading and arguing with them.

Just behind the policemen were Fazlı Hoca and Red Yaşar, both of whom had shops on the bridge; they fixed their blank eyes on the churning waters, heads in their hands. Their shops had been flooded, and now they were watching bolts of cloth bobbing and sinking in the furious currents. All the shops on the bridge had suffered the same fate, though the damage to Fazlı Hoca's shop was said to be the worst.

By the time we reached the bridge the sky had darkened. Supremely sure of herself, my grandmother went up to one of the policemen blocking the bridge. 'We're here,' she said. The policeman (the Commissar, I was told later) said something to his colleagues. Three of them approached us – their trouser legs were rolled up as far as the knee. The Commissar picked us up one by one and lifted us onto the three policemen's backs. We crossed the flooded bridge on piggyback; my grandmother walked alongside us barefoot, her shoes in her hand.

When we got home, we found our mother waiting for us in the street. She embraced us with joy. My grandmother had triumphed, once again, but – as was always the case – she didn't brag about it, and never mentioned that day again.

That night in our house there was much discussion as to how, when the bridge had been closed to all traffic, my grandmother had managed not just to cross the bridge but to convince three policemen to carry us. Even when my grandfather paid tribute to 'Sergeant Seher', she still showed no desire to dwell on it, and at once tried to change the subject. We crawled up onto our grandmother's lap, so that she could pat us on the back and pamper us a little more.

My grandmother spent her last days in my Aunt Zehra's house in Gebze.[10] It was Aunt Zehra's youngest son Emrah who gave the other children and grandchildren the news of her death, and as soon as we had heard, those of us who lived outside Gebze and Istanbul – in Ankara, Elazığ and Edremit – had to set out at once to make it to the funeral. We all gathered in Aunt Zehra's house.

Aunt Zehra's neighbours took a close interest in all arrivals, competing with each other to feed each newcomer, open their homes to us, and offer us beds.

We were moved and surprised by Aunt Zehra's neighbours' generosity. Whenever we tried to thank them, we got the same answer:

'Don't thank us. Aunt Seher was grandmother to us all. She was always such a helpful, generous, loving person. It is our duty to help her through her final journey, please don't deny this to us.'

Each one had a tale to tell about Seher's qualities.

Helpfulness was a quality that came naturally to her, and it was central to her character. She responded to those who needed help not out of a sense of duty, or because she felt obliged to do good works: she did so instinctively, because it was in her nature. The moment she heard that someone needed help, she would rush to their side to do whatever needed to be done. She refused to talk

10 An industrial town on the north coast of the Sea of Marmara.

about her acts of kindness, and if anyone else tried to do so, would recite the old proverb: 'Do someone a kindness, then throw it in the sea. If God doesn't appreciate it, the fish will.'

Her opinion was highly valued, and when her neighbours had had disagreements, they would ask her to arbitrate. If it was a dispute between a man and his wife, usually my grandfather would also be involved. She was forever being invited to other people's homes to resolve quarrels and restore the peace. My grandfather would sometimes accompany her, but generally he'd be sleeping or relaxing at home and so refused to go. Even if it meant staying up all night, my grandmother would always respond to anyone who needed her, anyone whose conflicts she might help resolve.

When she began to complain about having trouble with her eyes, my Uncle Mahmut took her to Ankara. He arranged for her to be operated on at the Eye Bank. She came out with two pairs of glasses – one for distance, and the other for close work. My uncle warned her that she needed to wear them all the time, and he asked us all to keep a close watch to make sure she did so. From that day on, the household's new job was to check every morning to make sure our grandmother was wearing her glasses, and if she wasn't, to find them and make her wear them. One morning there was a hunt for the glasses, and no one could find them. No corner of the house was left unsearched, and although my grandmother had evaded the first questions she was soon obliged to come clean. There was a widow living in the neighbourhood. The previous evening, she had come to visit my grandmother, and after saying that she, too, was having trouble with her eyesight, she tried on my grandmother's glasses and said, 'These glasses suit me perfectly, Sister Seher.' Whereupon my grandmother gave her neighbour her glasses and their case.

Her explanation was clear and concise. 'I can buy a new pair but she cannot. With Allah's blessing, may they bring her happy days.' That was all she would say; the subject was closed. My grandmother went without glasses for a long time after that because my uncle, who had her prescription, was out of the country. To get her another pair of glasses, we had to wait for my uncle to return from abroad, buy the glasses, and send them from Ankara.

This is why my grandfather would describe my grandmother as someone who provided 'cradles for the newborn and coffins for the dead,' and though her goodwill towards others made him proud, this didn't stop him complaining about it.

Prayers in the mosque had just come to an end and the congregation joined the prayers at my grandmother's funeral. In a loud voice, the *hoca* said, 'May God forgive her faults!' and 'Do you give her your blessing?', repeating each line three times. Those assembled in the courtyard replied, 'We give her our blessing!' Once again I couldn't stop myself: 'Let *her* give *us* her blessing,' I cried. 'May she forgive *us* – forgive you, forgive us, forgive us all.' I could not stop my voice from getting louder and louder. Everyone gave me puzzled looks; most understood nothing of what I said.

Heranuş had successfully completed her third year in school. Because she was a quick learner and a responsible child, she not only helped her mother with the housework but looked after the other children, playing with them, and trying to teach them what she had learned in school. Whatever task she undertook, she saw it through to the end.

One warm day in spring, the gendarmes raided the village. They assembled a group of villagers in the *meydan*, and there, in front of their eyes, slaughtered Nigoros Agha, the village headman, who spoke very good Turkish, and acted as negotiator between the villagers, the tax collectors and other local authorities. Later they rounded up all the grown men in the village and took them away. The gendarmes marched them off in pairs, each with his hand tied to his companion's. Among them were Heranuş's grandfathers and three of her uncles. The word was that these men were taken to Palu. But because they never returned from wherever it was they were taken, it is impossible to know exactly what happened.

The village was now made up of only women and children; having watched as all the men – young and old – were beaten with the butts of rifles, taunted, rounded up and marched away, they were seized with terror; they could not bring themselves to go back into their houses, they couldn't work – they just gathered together in the *meydan* to share their grief, to seek advice from the old people, and to argue. No one knew where or why the men had been taken away, but there were many rumours.

Heranuş's paternal grandmother kept telling the others, 'Don't worry, everything will work out fine, everyone will come back,' and then, 'You were children then, you don't know the half of it. Our village was raided just like this twenty years ago, the whole village was emptied. They sent us all into exile.'

Another woman interjected, 'Many people died on the roads, and on the mountains. We buried our dead in those mountains.'

Heranuş's grandmother continued her story:

'Some of us died, but most of us managed to survive on those mountains for a very long time. Then one day we received permission to return to our village, and this we did.

'When we returned, we found our churches, schools and houses burned and destroyed.

'It took a few years to rebuild our homes and schools, but as you can see we built each one to be stronger and more beautiful than before'. Several other women nodded in assent.

But most of the younger women were not as optimistic as Heranuş's grandmother. They insisted that this attack was not the same as the one of twenty years earlier, and that the men they'd taken away would never be coming back. In silence, Heranuş said every prayer she knew so that what her grandmother said might come true, that her grandfather and her uncles might return, and she tried to guess which mountain they'd been taken to. Like all the other children in the village, she gave her full attention to the conversations going on around her as she tried to figure out what had happened, and what was still to come.

Heranuş's mother İsguhı had been nine years old at the time of the exile to which her mother-in-law had referred, and it must have been her childhood experiences that made her foresee the dangers ahead before any of the others; assembling her sisters, she told them to cut off their hair, do everything to make their faces as ugly as they could, and find unbecoming clothing that would keep them from drawing attention to themselves.

All but the youngest, Siranuş, obeyed her; after gathering up their hair in five plaits and chopping each off, they went on to follow her other instructions. But not only did Siranuş refuse to cut her hair – neither would she make her face ugly or wear unflattering clothes.

On the evening of the day the men were taken, a raiding party swept into the village. They kidnapped all the beautiful young girls and women in the village. Siranuş was amongst them. There was no news of Siranuş or her fellow captives the next day, nor was there any in the days that followed. Those who'd seen Siranuş and the others being taken captive said that they had been caught by their plaits and bound by their hands and carried off like that.

When İsguhı discovered that the gendarmes had not raided some of the neighbouring villages – including, at that point, her sister-in-law's village – she took her three children, Heranuş, Horen and Hiyayr, and left for her sister-in-law's house. But before long the gendarmes came to this village, too, and this time they gathered up all the men and women and took them to Palu. Heranuş, her mother, and her two brothers were among them.

In Palu they separated the men from the women. They shut the women into the church courtyard. The men remained outside. Before long the women and children could hear blood-curdling screams from over the walls. Because the courtyard walls were very high, they could see nothing of what was happening on the other side. They stood there staring at each other; mothers, grandmothers, children were holding each other and shaking. The entire courtyard was trembling.

Heranuş and her brothers clung to their mother's skirts, but though she was terrified, she was desperate to know what was going on. Seeing that another girl had climbed onto someone's shoulders to see over the wall, she went to her side. The girl was still looking over the wall; when, after a very long while, she came down again, she said what she had seen. All her life, Heranuş would never forget what came from this girl's lips: 'They're cutting the men's throats, and throwing them into the river.'

After the cries had died away, the courtyard's massive double door swang open; the gendarmes then formed two lines and marched the women and children out of Palu. Here they said that they had permission to go back to their villages and that this meant they should all return immediately to their village of origin. They returned to their villages to find they'd been looted. The Muslim villagers in the area had wasted no time, stripping everything from their houses, right down to the beds and the quilts.

On returning home, the women realised that they could no longer afford the luxury of mourning for their men, but rushed straight to their fields and gardens in search of food for their empty stomachs. They worked together to gather enough of the crops that had ripened to feed themselves for a few days; they cracked the wheat on their rooftops to make cracked wheat; boiling it, they satisfied their hunger.

They had no chance to contemplate what to do next. The gendarmes came back to the village; announcing that all those present were to be sent into exile, including bedridden women. They ordered them to assemble at once. So began the long, agonising death march.

By the time they reached Çermik Hamambaşı, their numbers had dwindled. The ever-diminishing procession was to rest there and move on the next day. İsguhı was carrying her young son Hırayr in a bundle tied to her back. All the way, she had been so determined not to fall to the back of the line that she was almost running, holding her other two children's hands tight as she pulled and dragged them along. Many children had died along the way, but she had managed to bring her children safe and sound thus. Hunger, fatigue and silence had taken their toll, and they no longer had the strength to put one foot in front of the other. In the end they just collapsed on the ground.

The people of Çermik gathered around them, offering them food and water in exchange for their gold and jewellery. But these sunken-cheeked people had gone through all their money and valuables during the early days of the march and now had nothing left.

The crowd that had gathered around these miserable people grew steadily larger; some gazed in horror; others in loathing. A while later, some of these observers began to look at the children, and when one of them caught their eye they would seek out this child's relatives. A corporal on horseback, whom they later discovered was the commander of the Çermik gendarmes, asked for Heranuş, while Hıdır Efendi of Karamusa, a village connected to Çermik, asked for Horen. No one asked for Hırayr because he was too young. Despite her hunger and fatigue, İsguhı sprang up like a hawk and hid her children behind her. 'No one can take them from me. I'll never give them up.' She said these words as if she were challenging the entire world. İsguhı's mother Takuhi came over to her side and said that if she handed the children over to these men, they'd fare much better. Heranuş heard what her grandmother said as she tried to persuade İsguhı:

'My girl, the children are dying one by one. No one's going to come out of this march alive. If you give these men your children, you'll save their lives. If you don't, they'll die. We're all going to die. Let these children live, at least; give them to these men.'

Heranuş's aunt Zaruhi came in on the grandmother's side. She, too, thought Heranuş should be handed over to the corporal. Both these women tried everything they knew to persuade İsguhı, but she was adamant.

They were still arguing when the men pounced on them and grabbed Heranuş and Horen by their hands. İsguhı sprang forward with all her strength but the gendarme had already thrown Heranuş on his horse. İsguhı lunged for the horse, grabbing the gendarme's leg with one hand and Heranuş with the other, and pulled with all her might.

Seeing that he would not rid himself of this woman easily, the gendarme took out his whip and began to lash her with it. Despite the pain, İsguhı kept her hand firmly clamped around Heranuş's and tried to pull her child off the horse with every ounce of energy she could muster, alternately imploring and cursing the man, commanding him to give her back her daughter.

Then five-year-old Hırayr began to scream and cry. Thinking something terrible was happening to him, İsguhı turned for just one instant in the direction of the sound; at that very moment the corporal spurred his horse, which sprang forward and, as fast as an arrow, galloped off with Heranuş on its back.

And so the roads parted for İsguhı and Heranuş at Çermik Hamambaşı, never to come together again. As for five-year-old Hırayr, who had burst into tears because he feared the gendarme was about to kill his mother and his sister, and Heranuş's aunt and grandmother, who had said that 'we are all going to die', none were to come through this death march alive.

After suffering a massive heart attack, but, with the help of excellent care, coming through it, my grandfather exceeded expectations by agreeing to changes in his diet. On one winter day, however, his heart failed and he died. After my grandfather's death, and at the insistence of her children and grandchildren, my grandmother gave up her house and distributed her belongings. From this time on, she would divide her time amongst her children, going from house to house until her last days in Gebze. The only grandchild whose house she would stay in was Handan; she said she was very comfortable there, and whenever she made the trip from Elazığ to Edremit to Istanbul, she would stop off at Handan's house in Ankara, where she would prolong her stay as long as possible.

Handan had married at a very young age and devoted herself to being a housewife. I was sent to teacher training college, this being the easiest way to make a start in life so that I could begin to look after my family. I applied to schools in Ankara so that Haluk could continue at the university there, which was, as my mother put it, 'just in front of the house'. And so we came to live in Ankara. Until Haluk finished his studies, I took on extra work outside teaching hours. The year Haluk graduated, I took the university examination and won a place in the law faculty. When she heard that I had been accepted, my grandmother was very pleased. Once again I was in her good books. Though my political ideas and my adversarial stance against the system caused her worry, deep down she supported me and this, I think, increased her confidence in me.

Lately my grandmother's eyes had been bothering her; her sight was failing. Despite an operation and the glasses the doctors had given her – whose lenses were as thick as the bottom of a bottle – her eyesight was getting worse by the day.

It was such bad luck for a woman as tidy, industrious, quick-witted, and energetic as my grandmother to lose her eyesight. Thank God, the houses in which she stayed all met her standards of cleanliness. If she wore her thick glasses, she could just about find her way to the bathroom and the bedroom. 'My eyes have lost their lustre' was how my grandmother described it.

Every time we met, I would take her hand in mine, kiss it and say, 'Grandmother.' She would reply, 'Grandmother,' and then she would say my name and ask, 'Is it *you*?' Then, holding both my hands very tight, she would ask an endless string of questions. She'd never pass over a single detail and never forgot a thing; she wanted to know about everything. During these conversations of ours, she never once let go of my hands.

My grandmother had a very good memory. When she told us about something that had happened fifty years earlier, we were always amazed by the way she could remember the finest details. And she was very clever.

One day when I paid a visit to Handan's house, I heard that she was in the bedroom that belonged to my two nephews, Evrim and Özgür, who were at that time still in primary school. As I walked down the corridor, I could hear the conversation in that room; I stopped to listen. The boys were trying to recite a lesson, and my grandmother was correcting their mistakes and reminding them of the parts they'd left out. I carried on listening. Then Handan came out of the kitchen, and I signalled for her to be quiet; we carried on listening together. My grandmother was helping her great-grandchildren with their lessons. First the boys would read out the passage for their homework, and my grandmother would listen, and then the boys would close the book and try to recite from memory. Having heard the passage for the first and only time, my grandmother could remember every last word; she was able to correct the boys' mistakes, and fill in the details they had missed out. She would make them repeat the lesson until they had it perfect.

One day in 1975, when she was staying with us in Ankara, she said, 'If you're not busy, come sit with me, why don't you, I have something to tell you.' I went to sit with her and she took my hands between hers and said, 'Did you know? My mother, father and brother are all in America, and your uncle lost their address. If anyone can find them, you can. Find them for me, will you?'

I could tell from her monotone and her choice of words that it been a very difficult decision to speak to me. First I couldn't quite understand what she was saying.

'What are you saying, Grandmother? Do we now have relatives living in America?' I asked, mistakenly assuming she was joking.

But my grandmother was very serious. 'I don't know their address, but I do know that they live in America, in New York,' she said.

'So why did they go to America, Grandmother?'

'They just went, that's all.'

'When did they go there?'

'When I was a child.'

'Okay, then, why didn't they take you with them?'

'I was going to go later, but your Uncle Mahmut broke off relations. He lost their address.'

I was utterly bewildered. My head was full of questions but her answers made no sense to me. For days I tried to get her to tell me more, but I was not able to find out much beyond the fact that her real parents lived in America. We had always been told that my grandmother and grandfather were cousins. This wasn't true. We'd always been told that my grandmother was from Çermik. This wasn't true either. Much of what we had thought to be true turned out to be false.

But as I went in search of my grandmother's family, I was to learn many facts. I kept pressing my grandmother for more information, always making sure that I only did so when we were alone. At the time, I didn't discuss what she told me with anyone else, and neither did I discuss the shock waves it sent through my own life. I cannot say if this was because my grandmother wanted it this way, or if it came from my own shame, but I, too, hid what I was hearing from all others: my world had been turned upside down, my distress ran very deep, and I was trying to pull through it alone.

We formed a special and very secret alliance. I sensed her longing to rid herself of the burden she had been carrying all these years – to open the curtains that hid her secret, to tell this story she had never shared with a soul – but I think she also knew that, having gone through life knowing none of it, I would find it deeply upsetting. She was protecting me.

I did everything I could to encourage her. At last she began to speak. As she told her story, her voice would tail off, and it was only after my insistent questions that she would take her story up again. Though she related the events, she made no attempt to explain them, and she was especially reluctant to describe her thoughts or feelings.

'My name was Heranuş. My mother's name was İsguhı, and my father's name was Hovannes; he was living in America with my two uncles at the time. I had two brothers. They called my grandfather Hayrabed Efendi. His word was valued not just in our own village but throughout the area; everyone sought out his advice, that's the kind of man he was. Our village was a good size; it had three *muhtars*.[11] This was how she began.

11 An elected village authority.

She went on to tell me how the gendarmes had come to the village one day and taken away all the men, including her grandfather and her uncles; how her mother had taken refuge with her children in her sister-in-law's village; how the gendarmes had then come to that village, rounded up everyone, the women as well as the men, and taking them to Palu; how they'd cut the men's throats and thrown them into the river; how the river had run with blood for days on end; and how the women and children had been marched away from their homes and into exile.

'During the march, my mother was so anxious to avoid the back of the line that she walked very fast, and because we couldn't keep up with her, she pulled us with her hands. At the back of the line we could hear people crying, screaming, pleading. Every time this happened, my mother would walk a little faster, to keep us from looking over our shoulders. On the evening of the first day of the march, two of my aunts came running from the back to catch up with us, and they were crying hysterically.'

My grandmother stopped here. She took a deep breath. I kissed her hand. She continued.

'My aunt – my uncle's wife – was ill, and she couldn't walk, so the gendarmes killed her with a bayonet. They threw her body to the side of the road.'

'Grandmother, was she the wife of your father's brother?'

'No. She was the wife of my mother's brother, and she was pregnant.'

'The elderly, the infirm, the ones who couldn't walk – throughout the march they'd kill them with their bayonets and leave them lying there, just where they fell. They left them lying there, unprotected, on the mountaintops.'

As she told me this agonising, barely believable story, I noticed that my grandmother would not look me in the eye, that instead she fixed her eyes on a point on the carpet; that while she held my left hand tight she kept making the same movement with her right hand, passing over her thigh, as if she were ironing her dress, smoothing out the wrinkles, over and over, without realising she was doing so. Realising that it must be very tiring for her to tell this story, I tried to think how I might give her a break. She was very fond of frothy coffee. So I asked, 'Grandmother, would you like me to make you a coffee?' She didn't hear me. She kept doing this thing with her hand, as she rocked very gently back and forth. I took her right hand in mine and kissed it. I asked again. This time she heard me. 'Your coffee is good and frothy, so yes, why don't you make me some.'

When I brought back her coffee, I saw that she had raised her head, looking up at the ceiling in the way people do when they are trying to remember something. When she saw me, she at once beckoned to me to sit down next to her. What this woman had lived through defied belief and after burying these memories for so many years, it taxed her brain to put them into words, to tell the story. I put the coffee cup into her hands and she continued:

'After crossing the bridge at Maden – at Havler – my grand-mother threw two of her grandchildren into the water. These were my uncle's daughters. They'd lost both their mother and their father, and they couldn't walk. One of the children sank right away but the other child's head bobbed up in the water. My grandmother – my father's mother – pushed her head back underwater. The child's head popped out of the water again, and this was the last he saw of the world, for my grandmother pushed him back under again. . . Then she threw herself into the madly rushing water and disappeared from sight.'

Here my grandmother stopped. That this part of the story had affected her deeply was clear from the way she kept returning to it to tell it again. In the coming years, she would refer to this incident many times, and each time the story would end with a deep silence.

My grandmother then went on to tell me what had happened during their stopover in Çermik Hamambaşı; how her mother had refused to take advice from her own sister and mother; how her mother had refused to give up her children; how she had been taken away by force.

'They took me to a garden. It was brilliant green, like the gardens in our village. The trees were full of fruit. There was a stream passing through the middle of the garden and its water was crystal clear. There were eight other girls from my village in that garden; all of them had been taken the way I'd been.'

'They filled our stomachs with hot food, and they gave us permission to pick fruit from the trees. After a while I got it into my head that I had to see my mother, and they promised to take me to her. After that we played in the garden. We plucked pears and apples from the trees, drank the ice-cold water from the stream.'

On the evening of that same day, the girls in the garden were taken one by one to separate houses. And the gendarme commander came to the garden to collect Heranuş. Heranuş did not want to go with him. 'I began to cry, saying "I miss my mother!", and I cried all through that night until morning.

'They saw that this wasn't working, so the next morning they took me to Hamambaşı. I went there, and it was completely empty; there was no one there. I could see that they had taken my mother and the others away; they had kept me all night and brought me back in the morning to dash my hopes. I found out that my mother and the others had moved on in the direction of Siverek. After that, I would look at the mountains of Siverek every day and cry.'

The doorbell rang; there were people coming. My grandmother stopped her story there. And anyway, I did not have the strength to hear much more. It was hard to keep myself from running out into the street to cry and scream. I would never have believed any of this, unless it was my grandmother telling me.

What she told me did not fit with anything I knew. It turned the known world on its head, smashing my values into a thousand pieces. I no longer knew how I felt; and as inchoate thoughts chattered and throbbed and swirled through my mind, I gave in to a deep dread that threatened to engulf everything and everyone.

Whether my eyes were open or closed, certain images would not go away: the crowd huddled in the church courtyard, and especially the pupils of the children's eyes; the babies who'd been thrown into the water, and their fight to live, their heads bobbing up in the water; the moment when Heranuş was snatched from her mother's arms. . . And then, after seeing all these things, I would remember the poems I recited for national holidays.

Because I was one of the best students in the class, my teachers would ask me to read out heroic poems on every national holiday. I would recite these poems about our 'glorious past' at the top of my voice, and with such passion; but now I could not remember this without seeing the children's eyes opened wide with terror, and their heads disappearing into the water, and the river that ran red with blood for days.

I did not sleep at all that night. The next day I wandered about like a ghost. My grandmother and I were not alone in the house that day; we couldn't speak.

It was during this time that I remembered one thing my grandmother had said. When we were children, we were very afraid of cemeteries, and we'd all try to scare each other with terrifying stories about cemeteries and ghosts. The Maden cemetery was on the way to the gardens we used to go to for picnics.

Seeing our fear as we passed the cemetery, my grandmother would say, 'Don't fear the dead, children, no one can hurt them anymore. Evil comes from the living, not the dead.' When my grandmother said this to us, was she thinking of the things she had just told me? I couldn't find it in me to ask, but I am almost certain that she was.

*   *   *

From that day on, an alliance formed between my grandmother and me that no one else knew about; we shared a secret, and this kept us close until the day she died.

There was a lot of coming and going during this period. It was a long while before my grandmother and I had a chance to speak again. Perhaps this was for the best. It gave me a chance to absorb what she had told me and to resolve to some degree the contradictory thoughts her story had provoked.

One day, when I found my grandmother alone in the house again, I took her hands into mine, kissed her soft cheeks, and asked her to continue the story where she had left off. Without a moment's pause, she began to speak:

'The man who took me was Corporal Hüseyin, the commander of the Çermik gendarme headquarters. His wife's name was Esma. Though they dearly wanted children, they'd not been able to have any. Hüseyin – bless his soul, and may Allah show him an abundance of mercy – was a good man. He had as much power as a major. He considered me his child and looked after me very well.

'They used to call him a soft-hearted man. They had massacred the Armenians of Çermik, too, and thrown them into a bottomless well. There's a waterhole between Çermik and Çüngüş that they call Duden, and they say it has no bottom. After cutting off their heads, they threw the Armenians into this Duden. Colonel Hüseyin was there for the massacre of the men, but he refused to take part in it when they threw in the women and children; he refused to obey orders. They said he'd been punished for this.'

Unable to bear it any longer, I broke in:

'Grandmother, if Corporal Hüseyin was as soft-hearted as they say, wouldn't it have pained him at all to see the men slaughtered and thrown into the well?'

This was what my grandmother said, after pausing to think: 'How should I know?'

She did not give me a chance to ask her again. She continued with her story. It was clear to me that she loved Colonel Hüseyin very dearly, and that she did not wish to ask questions about him, or to let others do so.

'They gave me the name "Seher". I learned Turkish quickly. I did whatever they asked.

'But Esma Hanım could never manage to accept me.

'Colonel Hüseyin wanted me to call him father. He was very happy whenever I called him father. "Call me father again, my girl," he'd say.

'One day a neighbour's child cursed my father in the street. I got very angry, and I cursed *his* father using the same word. This child's mother came to the house to complain that night, to say that I had used a swearword. After the woman left, Colonel Hüseyin called me to his side. I went with my shoulders bowed, expecting a punishment. He pulled me to his side and said, "So tell me, my girl, what happened today?" And I said that, actually, that child had cursed *my* father first, and that it was after this that I had said, "Actually it is *your* father who's the . . ." and used the same curse word. My story pleased him no end. After laughing heartily, he said, "That's splendid, my girl. So now tell me again – what was it you said?"

'So I told him again. And he repeated the story many, many times, that day and the days that followed. And every time, after he'd laughed, he'd stroke my hair and say, "You've done me proud, my girl."

'One holiday, Colonel Hüseyin came home with material for two silk dresses; Esma Hanım and I greeted him by kissing his hand. He opened the package in his hand and showed us the two pieces of material, which had been made from the same bolt of silk, saying, "Look what I've brought you."

'When Esma Hanım saw that he had bought dresses made of the same silk, she was so angry and jealous that she said these very words: "If maids and servant girls wear silk, then what is the lady of the house to wear?"

'So that was how I found out I was a servant girl. Colonel Hüseyin was furious at his wife. Throwing the material to the floor, he shouted, "That Sultan Reşat – and may Allah strike him blind – he turned every whining ninny into a lady, and he made brilliant children their servants." Whereupon he left the house, not returning until the evening.'

It had wounded my grandmother deeply to be called a servant girl. She told me about this incident and others like it many times over. Each time she felt the wound as keenly as she had felt it that day, when she'd first heard it, and this is how her story continued:

'So this is how I found out that I was supposed to be a servant girl. I was a girl from a family that had seen the world; I was the apple of my mother's eye, and my father's precious jewel. And now I was a servant girl, and how I cried inside, how I grieved every night. Even if Colonel Hüseyin treated me like his daughter, I was still a servant girl.'

With a painful smile, my grandmother continued:

'Then, another day, another child and I got into an argument – she was trying to take some bread from my hand and I didn't want to give it to her. When she threw a stone at me, I pushed her; she fell on the ground and began to cry. Her mother came out and called to Esma Hanım. "Esma Hanım, Esma Hanım," she said. "Could you come out and take charge of this servant girl of yours? She's beating up the children."'

My grandmother went on to tell me that Esma Hanım really did treat her like a servant; that she couldn't bear seeing how fond her husband was of Seher; that, once my grandmother had blossomed into a young woman, she began to fear that her husband would take her for his wife, and that at this point she became very jealous and treated her very badly. Because she'd not been able to have children, she'd always feared that he might take a second wife.

'And so this is how it happened, my girl; as you know, the good die young. And Colonel Hüseyin died young.'

After Colonel Hüseyin died, she went through more hard times. But instead of telling me about them, she said only this:

'There were eight of us altogether – eight girls from the same village, all of us living now in Çermik. Each of us was in a separate house. The women used to say to me, "You're the unluckiest of us all."'

And Horen, who'd been taken off by Hidir Efendi, of Karamusa Village – he was not Horen anymore, but Ahmet. Because he worked as a shepherd, they called him 'Ahmet the Shepherd.' One day, when Ahmet the Shepherd came to Çermik to visit the market, one of the girls from Habab saw him and recognised him. She told him about his sister's new home, family and name. The news reached Ahmet the Shepherd's sister Seher with the same speed.

The two children asked to see each other. But Esma Hanım would not grant my grandmother permission to see her brother. She couldn't stop them meeting, however.

'Esma Hanım didn't want me and Horen seeing each other. She wouldn't let him in the house, but we still managed to see each other. Every time he came to town, we'd meet in secret, we'd talk.'

From that day on, whenever they met in secret, brother and sister would share every scrap of news they had about their mother. They discovered that the survivors of the march had been sent to Aleppo. Though there was no hard information about who had or had not survived the march, rumours abounded. My grandmother described the most widespread rumour with these words: 'They said that in the Urfa desert, an order came to kill them. They took the survivors to Aleppo.'

After a short pause, she told me about meeting her aunt:

'One day I was sweeping the front of the house. A woman came up and stopped in the street outside. I lifted my head and looked at her. She collapsed on the ground, racked with sobs.

This woman, dressed in the colourful *kofik* clothing of the Kurds of the region, was my Aunt Siranuş, who had been carried off in that raid.'

Overcome by curiosity and excitement, I bombarded her with questions: 'Who were the men who kidnapped Siranuş, where did they take her, how did she track you down?'

Either my grandmother did not want to tell me who had kidnapped Siranuş, and what she had gone through thereafter, or she didn't know. She left all my questions unanswered, saying only this:

'She had married a Kurd from Siverek, and her life was comfortable.'

Returning to her meetings with her aunt, she continued her story. Her aunt had followed every lead, spoken to everyone she could, asked questions, and when she found that her niece was in Çermik, had gone to see her, weighed down with gifts. Aunt and niece embraced at the door; swaying back and forth, they had cried very loudly. They were still crying when Esma Hanım came to the door. Refusing to admit the aunt or her presents, she sent her away.

Suddenly a vague memory came back to me from childhood. We were in Maden. A visitor came with her grandson. They said she was my grandmother's aunt. I can remember her rosy cheeks and her charming, beautiful face even today. And also her many layered, multicoloured velvet clothes. In order to be sure, I asked:

'In Maden, when we were living in the house over the fountain, the visitor who came with her grandson . . .'

'Yes, after I married your grandfather, we saw a great deal of each other.'

I remembered another detail about my grandmother and her aunt. This red-cheeked woman asked if her son might ask for Aunt Sabahat's hand in marriage. She tried very hard to persuade my grandmother, but to no avail. My grandmother's answer was clear, short and definite: 'I am not giving my daughter to a relative!'

When my grandfather's relations made the same request, my grandmother's response, in spite of her husband's best efforts, was the same: 'I'm not giving my daughter to a relative!'

Esma Hanım's older sister died at a very young age, as did her sister's husband. At the age of fifteen, her nephew Fikri was left motherless and fatherless with no prospects and no means of support. Fikri was a lazy, irresponsible boy who could not hold down a job. They married him off to my grandmother, thinking she would know how to handle a boy who was inclined to spend his time with the town layabouts. According to the register (but only the register) my grandmother, the daughter of Hüseyin and Esma, was marrying her cousin; one was fifteen, the other sixteen.

'After your Uncle Mahmut came into the world, your grand-father went to do his military service. After he returned, he came back to the house one day huffing and puffing. "I have some good news for you, so make sure you have something good for me, too." I was filled with excitement and fear. "May it serve us well, please God," I said. "Your father has written a letter, he sent it to your brother. Your brother will be bringing the letter over tomorrow."

'That night I was so overjoyed and excited that I couldn't sleep. Horen came the next day, and when he took the letter from his pocket my heart was pounding so hard that I thought it was going to burst. He took the letter out of the pocket of his work-clothes and he smoothed it open. We both looked at the letter but could understand nothing. The letter was written in the old, Armenian script. Hediye Hanım could read the old writing, and we got her to decipher it for us. We discovered what had happened to our mother, and how she had managed to find our father; we also heard that our father had now come to Aleppo from America to find us.'

'According to the man who had brought us the letter, our father had been in Aleppo for some time. He'd been looking for us, and had employed smugglers to help find us.

'The man who had brought the letter worked as a smuggler on the Syrian-Turkish border; now he waited to take our answer back to our father. We had a letter written in the new alphabet and gave it to this man to send.

'After some time had passed, a new letter arrived from our father, and with it he sent us money. He wanted us to come to Aleppo.

'For days I pleaded with your grandfather, and in the end we agreed to go there together. By now, your mother had been born. We prepared for the journey.

'We sold our animals and gathered up our things, but then his aunt, who had some authority in the family, managed to change your grandfather's mind. "Be careful, my boy – they'll take their daughter away, and abandon you here with your children. On no account should you go." With all her cajoling she managed to scare him.

'His aunt then persuaded other members of the family to put pressure on him, so in the end grandfather decided not to go and not to send me either. As you know, your dear departed grandfather was simple, gullible. So I stayed, but Horen went. He had to spirit himself across the border to Aleppo, going with the smugglers who had been working with my father. When I said goodbye to him I felt as if I had sent him away with the last piece of my heart.

'Years passed, and I'd lost all hope, when a letter came from Horen. He had managed to find our father and together they'd gone to America. We began to exchange letters. They sent photographs, and we called a photographer to the house to have our pictures taken, too, and we sent them some photographs. The year your Uncle Mahmut finished lycée, they sent money in a letter, so that I could buy a plane ticket to visit them in America.

Marseilles, en route to America, *c.* 1928–1929. Horen is standing on the far left, wearing a new watch and chain. Hovannes is seated in front of him.

This photograph accompanied Horen's first letter from America to his sister. İsguhı is standing on the far left, back row, and next to her is Horen. Seated in the middle are Hovannes and his brother Hrant.

"If nothing else, just come for a few months," they said, "so we can see you."

'That summer, your uncle went in my place. My parents had been expecting me to come, and when they saw your uncle instead, they were very disappointed, and reproached him: "We were expecting your mother, why didn't you bring her with you?"

'Horen and my American-born sister entertained him royally; they took him to see the sights and said they would like him to continue his studies in America. But after an argument with them, your uncle broke off contact with all of them; when he came back, he said, "I've lost their address," and stopped me getting in touch with them. We've never been in touch since, but I remember their names, and the city they lived in. If I give you this information, can you find them for me?

'Why didn't you go, grandmother? They sent you that money so that *you* could go!'

'I had no birth certificate and no passport. They said it would be very hard for me to leave the country. One day your uncle came to the house. "I've got myself a passport," he announced; "I'm going to America." And I replied that, as much as I would like to go, it seemed impossible for me to do so. But at least my son should go and kiss my mother's and father's hands.'

'You didn't need someone else to get you a birth certificate and a passport. If you'd wanted it, you could have done it, grand-mother. Why didn't you try?'

'How should I know?'

Whenever she did not want to explain something, whenever she wanted to avoid an argument, my grandmother would always give the same answer: 'How should I know?' Every time she said these words, it seemed to me that she was saying, 'You're right, I so longed to go; but I was helpless, so what could I do?'

She was a woman who had endured unimaginable hardship throughout her life; if ever her children or those close to her faced

This photograph accompanied the family's letter from
Turkey to Horen in America. At the bottom, my
grandfather wrote my grandmother's words:
'A family memento for my brother, 5/9/1949. Seher.'

an obstacle, she did everything in her power to help them overcome it. So why, when it came to the question of her true identity, did she feel so helpless? Why could she not defend her identity, or the family into which she had been born? Why couldn't she stand by her own wishes?

With time, I realised that my mother and aunts knew most of this painful story. But she had never told them about the inhuman crimes she had witnessed; I was the only one who knew of them. It was with me that she shared the details that had most pained and affected her. I think she could no longer bear to keep them to herself.

Later I spoke with my mother, asking her why my uncle had broken off relations with the family. My mother related my uncle's side of the story:

'After staying there two or three months, when your uncle said he was ready to go home, they told him he should stay there to continue his education. When your uncle refused, his grandfather got angry and declared, "If you were always planning to go back, why did you bother to come? We didn't send that money so that you could come over for the grand tour. If nothing else, your mother could have used this money to buy herself a house." Your uncle was so angered by these words that he decided to break off all relations.

'If what he said was true, your uncle was in the wrong. When he first came back, he said, "As soon as I finish my education, as soon as it's humanly possible, I'm sending them back their money." But he then forgot his promise. We pleaded with him, but he wouldn't give us the address – he said he'd lost it. He was very angry with them. If you ask me, your uncle behaved very selfishly. He did not think about our mother at all.'

I asked my mother why grandmother had hidden the truth from us.

'Your grandmother didn't tell us anything either, my girl. We found out from what other people told us, and in the course of events,' she said.

'What events?'

'When we were children, we'd sometimes get into fights with the other children in the neighbourhood. When they got mad at us, they'd call us "convert's spawn". When they called us this, your grandmother would be beside herself. Whenever she heard this, she would throw a scarf over her head and go straight to see the neighbours. She argued, reasoned, sometimes spoke sweetly and sometimes lost her temper; but the long and the short of it was that the neighbourhood children stopped calling us "convert's spawn" when they were angry.'

'Did they forget you were converts?'

'They didn't forget – they just stopped using the word. They said nothing. And as for us, we never mentioned it again,' she said, adding, 'We didn't know what the word "convert" meant, and this is how we found out. The story in the town was that our mother was Armenian and that her parents had gone to America and left her here. But whenever we brought this up inside the family, the subject was closed so quickly that we realised it was not to be discussed, and so we never talked about it.'

Then my mother told me what had happened to my uncle when he went to military school:

'Your uncle was very eager to continue his studies, but your grandfather said, "I can't support all these people by myself. What good will an education do him? I can't afford it anyway; let him work instead and bring us in some money." Your grandfather did not have steady employment and we had to struggle to make ends meet, so your uncle decided to enrol in a military boarding school that gave scholarships. He prepared his documents and applied, but despite the fact that he was an excellent student, this school refused to take him.'

'Why?'

'Because of a word on your grandmother's birth certificate: *Muhtedi*.'

'What does *muhtedi* mean?'

'*Muhtedi* is a word for people who become Muslims later on. In other words, it means convert.'

This affair with the school upset my mother a great deal.

'Aunt Zehra's father-in-law, Kazım Efendi, may he rest in peace, was for a time the director of the birth registrations office in Maden; when he was in charge, he changed my mother's birth certificate. She didn't ask on her own behalf, but wanted it altered so that she could protect her children from harm.'

We lost our uncle at quite a young age. When he died, he was a deputy in the National Assembly. Though from time to time he criticised the state in superficial ways, throughout his life he stayed within the bounds it set, never deviating from its official ideology. Yet it was that same state that had refused to admit him to military school.

When I asked my grandmother about the military school refusing my uncle, I noticed that she was still distressed about it. She sighed and said, 'He always had perfect marks. He finished school with top grades, but still they wouldn't let him into the military. Kazım Efendi, may God show him mercy, may his resting place be bathed with heavenly light – after this happened, he changed my birth certificate.' But that was all she would say. The pain hadn't gone away.

We buried my grandmother, covered her with wet, cold earth, and returned together to my aunt's house. All day, people had been coming and going. Every room in the house had filled, even the kitchen and the balconies, and then emptied again. Once more the neighbours made us food and brought it over to my aunt's, set the table, and invited us all to sit down. The old women gathered together in one room to pray with their beads. By late afternoon people began to leave in ones and twos, and towards evening, our numbers had dwindled enough for us all to fit into the sitting room. We settled in there and talked until late. Aunt Zehra's husband's sister, Methiye Abla, turned to me at one point and said, 'Do you know, my mother-in-law was like your grand-mother.' What she meant by this was that her mother-in-law had also been taken from the death march by a Muslim family. When she saw my interest, she continued:

'Hacı's grandfather (Hacı was her husband's name) took two girls and one boy off the march, and brought them up. My mother-in-law was one of them. Years later, after she had married and her son was grown up, a man tracked them down one day. He asked to see my mother-in-law, but they would not let him. The man had a lot of money; it was my mother-in-law's inheritance, he said, and he'd come from a long way to give it to her, but it was no use. Haci wouldn't take the money either, and turned the man away. The man was going to come back but they had scared him so much that no other relative approached my mother-in-law again.'

Unable to help myself, I said, 'If you ask me, the person who was more frightened than anyone was Uncle Hacı.' She did not reply, but nodded her assent. After that, we retreated into our thoughts. After a pregnant silence, I was reluctant to let the matter pass, and asked:

'Couldn't your mother-in-law have said to her son, "What business is it of yours, this is my inheritance, it's my right?"'

Methiye Abla said, 'No, my dear, of course she couldn't; she said nothing, she couldn't say a thing.'

'Okay, but so many years had passed, and these women had faced death and survived, so why were they still so fearful? Did they not long for their real families, or were they afraid to do so?' I asked.

Methiye Abla's answer was very familiar. She thought for a while and then, to show me how helpless she was, she turned up the palms of her hands.

'Dear God, how should I know?'

We stayed up late that night, talking about how it must have affected them to live with such prejudice, to suffer such pressure and fear. Methiye Abla told us how her older brother, also called Hacı, had fallen in love with my aunt, and how this news was received at home.

'We were neighbours in Maden. We lived just across the street from each other. The two families were close. Before long, people began to talk about my brother's involvement with your aunt. My father loved your aunt, and your whole family, very much. "We're going to bring their girl into our family, Zehra will be my daughter-in-law," he'd say, and the thought made him happy. But my mother and the rest of the family didn't want her.'

As she said these words, I looked over at Aunt Zehra, who found an excuse to go into the kitchen. As Methiye Abla continued with her story, Zehra came in and out of the kitchen; she could overhear our conversation but didn't join in.

'They opposed the marriage, saying "Don't contaminate the race, don't spoil our pure blood." According to them, both your grandmother and Zehra were not racially pure. However, my father put his foot down and they went to ask for Zehra's hand in marriage. But', she said, 'imagine what happened?' Curious, we pressed her to contine. Methiye Abla smiled and went on:

'Before long, your uncle Hacı wanted to marry *me*. His mother was an Armenian convert, too; his mother had not come back from Armenia either. And as the saying goes, if you do a bad deed it will come back to haunt you. These people who didn't want a daughter-in-law with "impure blood" ended up handing their own daughter over to a husband with "impure blood". Anyway, shall I tell you something? In the place where we come from, it's hard to find anyone without "impure blood" – there's no one with any other kind.'

After I had heard my grandmother's story, my mind was in turmoil. How to find her relations in America? How to expose these hypocrisies, and bring the truth out into the open? I had still not found a way, I was still crushed under the weight of what I'd discovered on 12 September 1980, when there was a coup d'état.

Certain prominent people were so eager to purge the country that they chose to sacrifice their own children. So hungry were they for victims, they dispatched wave after wave of young people to the torture chambers – but even this didn't chill them.

Tens of thousands of households were scorched and destroyed by this squall, ours included. There were trials – people went to prison, or became fugitives; my uncle died, and immediately after, my mother; and so the years passed.

My mother, like my uncle, left us at a relatively young age. She was 59. It was very hard to bear her suffering. Because of the turmoil after the coup, it had been a long time since I'd seen her, and I missed her. It was with terrible longing that I counted the days until we would be together again; then I received news of her death.

Thinking that she might not have the strength to bear the loss of a second child, we hid my mother's death from my grand-mother for some time. But she found out in the end, and though she tried to keep a brave face, did not move from her prayer rug for days. She prayed and prayed, kneeling on the rug and crying, imploring the Creator to take her too. It was around this time that she had a very painful case of shingles, which affected her entire back and her abdomen; she could not rid herself of this agonising affliction for quite some time.

During the year that my own 'September storm' began to abate, I met Ayşe. Ayşe worked in America, where she had lived for years. We quickly became friends. I told her my grandmother's story and she was very affected by it.

I noticed that her eyes filled with tears as she listened, and that she had to struggle to keep herself from crying. Thinking I could trust her, I asked for her help. Ayşe agreed without hesitation and asked me for whatever information I had. I gave her the names. She went back to America.

Only a day after her departure, I was already waiting for Ayşe's phone call. Though I knew that it was a difficult thing she'd undertaken, my impatience grew as the days went on. But it wasn't long before Ayşe rang. In her excitement she was hardly able to breathe; she kept choking, as if her throat was blocked, and then she'd right herself.

After returning to America, she had gone in search of the Gadaryan family. Using the simplest, best-known channel, she'd tracked down a distant relation.

'After following a few leads that got me nowhere, I turned to the most obvious solution. I picked up the New York phone directory and called the first Gadaryan listed in it. That person who answered turned out to belong to the new generation, American born and bred. This distant relation remembered hearing Heranuş's story as a child. He didn't recognise any of the names I gave him, but promised to make enquiries and ring me back.'

I could hardly believe my ears. We had found my grandmother's family. I wanted to visit my grandmother at once to tell her what Ayşe had told me, but then decided against it and waited to hear more from Ayşe. My grandmother was in Ankara at the time, staying with Handan.

A short while later, Ayşe rang again. Her voice was shaking. She'd spoken a few times on the phone with Horen's daughter Virginia:

'Do you know, the day you and I spoke about Heranuş in Istanbul, Horen had a stroke. Because he was home alone, they couldn't get him treatment right away. Right now he's in hospital. His mind is still good; they told him that his sister had tried to reach him, and he cried. It's such bad luck, isn't it?'

'You're right, Ayşe, it's enough to make a person believe in fate.'

'Oh, and before I forget, there's something else. Horen named one of his daughters "Heranuş".'

I went to Ankara. I told my grandmother about Ayşe's conversations with Horen's daughter Virginia. It was only after telling her everything else that – with the greatest reluctance – I told her Horen had suffered a stroke and was now being looked after in hospital.

She listened to me carefully, calmly, and without interruption; only her red cheeks betrayed her emotions. When she learned that her brother was in hospital, her first question was about his state of health. I hadn't intended to, but suddenly I was spouting lies:

'Uncle Horen is recovering nicely, he's responded well to treatment. The doctors are hopeful.'

After murmuring a few things so softly that I couldn't hear them, she said:

'My eyes aren't good – I can't go, but tell him, the moment he gets out of hospital, he should jump on a plane and come, so that I can see him.'

I didn't know how to respond. Silently cursing myself, and wanting to change the subject at once, I said:

'Grandmother, did you know? Your brother Horen named one of his daughters after you.'

'Now how would I know that?'

'He gave her your name, grandmother; he named his daughter Heranuş.'

Then suddenly her eyes brightened, and a smile spread across her face. 'So they didn't forget us,' she said.

She grew so excited as she uttered these words that she began to choke, and it was some time before she found her voice again.

She asked no more questions, and tried hard to hide her feelings, but that day was the first time I ever heard my grandmother humming Turkish folk songs to herself. My grandmother was singing Turkish folk songs – so softly that I could catch neither the words nor the tune.

Towards evening, Haluk joined us. Together with my nephews, we now made a big, noisy group. All evening long, my grandmother teased us, cracked jokes, gave us impish smiles. We were happily surprised: we were not used to seeing our grandmother like this.

That day and the next, she would spring to her feet every time the phone rang, in the way that had once made my grandfather call her 'Sergeant Seher' or 'Mistress Storm', and go to pick it up. But even if she reached it first, she would wait for someone else to come and answer, and would then listen attentively to the conversation, to work out who it was at the other end of the line. Handan and Haluk noticed this change in her, too.

The moment the phone rang, she'd almost fly from her chair, landing in front of the phone before anyone else could get to it. I think she was expecting a call from America.

The phone call never came. Uncle Horen died in hospital. And for some unknown reason his daughters stopped talking to Ayşe. In spite of our entreaties, they did not call my grandmother; instead they broke off all contact.

I did not know what to tell my grandmother. In fact, she never asked me anything, never uttered a word, but whenever we met, would look into my face in a way that made me feel like bursting into tears and imploring, begging her to forgive me. This, too, I delayed too long, and this, too, I knew to be my fault; I felt so guilty I couldn't meet my grandmother's gaze.

After this last attempt to make contact, my grandmother never spoke of the matter again: there was nothing more to say. She'd lost the last person in her family whom she knew. She didn't talk about the rest. The subject was closed.

But every time I saw her, she would take my hands between hers, and then she would talk and talk about the old days. When we hadn't seen each other for a while, the moment she set eyes on me, she would hurry to tell me about the new details that had come back to her; usually she would forget what she had told me, and related the same stories again and again.

While she remembered vividly things that had happened long ago – even the smallest details – her short-term memory was always playing games with her.

One day she told me about a painful event from her childhood:

'But Grandmother,' I exclaimed fearfully, 'how can the things these people did fit in with the tenets of Islam?' This was what scared me: while she was telling me all these things, she said nothing about religion, offered no explanation or analysis, and continued to invoke the Creator like the most devout Muslim.

Without hesitation, she said:

'What they did doesn't square with Islam or any other religion.' What she said next was what she repeated at the end of every painful story. 'May those days go away, and may they never return.'

She paused, and thought, and then she told me something that Nermin Hanım, Handan's neighbour, had said. Once again, she avoided giving her own explanation by telling me how someone else saw it. Nermin Hanım and her whole family were very fond of my grandmother. Nermin and her mother were both very religious, the sort who prayed five times a day. They were from Erzıncan and had suffered throughout the Erzıncan earthquake:[12]

'In Erzıncan (Nermin Hanım told my grandmother) there were many Armenians. During the days of slaughter, when they were being deported, the Armenian women told the Muslims, "These lands will bring you no bounty! You won't hold on to them, you'll never know peace in these lands!"

'The years passed and lo and behold, one day the city of Erzıncan was struck by an earthquake. When it had finished, not a single stone stood on top of another. Thousands died. So that was when the Muslims turned to each other and said, "The Armenians' curse came true."'

12 The 1939 Erzıncan earthquake measured 7.8 on the Richter scale, and killed approximately 32,000 people.

Just as she was finishing high school, Handan's eldest daughter Ülgen – whom I loved dearly, and called 'Kitty' – fell in love with a boy. Handan was not against the match, but gave her consent on condition that her daughter should finish university before they married.

The prospective groom had won over my grandmother; the union met with her approval. And she tried to convince Handan that the children should marry right away. Almost every day, she would find an excuse to mention it, and to ask whether the wedding date had been set. Finally she explained why:

'I'd like to become a *toruntaht* before I die.'

To become a *toruntaht* was to live long enough to see your grandchild's grandchild; according to a popular belief, anyone who lived long enough to hold a grandchild's grandchild in his or her arms went straight to heaven. The moment they held that infant in their arms, they were cleansed of all sin. So to become a *toruntaht* was a rare blessing that Allah bestowed only on those vassals he loved most.

My grandmother was asking her granddaughter's daughter to marry at once and so make her a *toruntaht*, thus opening the gates of heaven for her. Before she finished university, Ülgen married.

As old and weak as she was, my grandmother wanted to be at the wedding, and she arrived in excellent spirits; as the guest of honour, she was given the best seat, and watched the proceedings with rapt attention from start to finish. At one point the band gave up its place to us, her grandchildren. We began to play and sing. My grandmother was beside herself with joy. When the microphone passed to Haluk we all began to clap, chanting 'Haluk! Haluk!'

Though Haluk has an exceptional voice and a fine ear, he holds it back; it takes a lot to get him to sing. Whenever we were having a party and in high spirits, we would plead with him to sing. When my grandmother heard Haluk's name, she began to clap and say, 'Please, I beg you! I beg you!' When he saw my grandmother clapping, Haluk took the microphone without anyone having to persuade him. As he sang, my grandmother was so ecstatic that she did something she had never done before – she asked Haluk to sing a Turkish folksong for her. It was the song called 'Dersim':

> Dersim, inside four mountains
> My rose in a copper jug
> May God look after Dersim
> I have a wound inside.
>
> O what has become of my master?
> His wilted, yellowed skin as pale as death
> After my master left
> This land turned to ruin
>
> With six unripe melons
> Dersim, let us go to Harput and back
> May your hand be in mine
> As we beg from door to door
>
> Oh help us, help us
> Why not ask for help?
> May your hand be in mine
> Why not three months on the road?

Grandmother swayed from side to side, beating time with her hand as she listened to the song. When it was over, she called Haluk to her side and kissed him twice on each cheek.

After the wedding, she did not have to wait long. My grandmother became a *toruntaht*. She took Handan's grandchild into her arms, and embraced Baby Ege as we took pictures. She seemed blissfully happy.

By now my grandmother was very old. She visited Aunt Sabahat in Elazığ, and remained there for an extended stay. While she was there, I didn't see her at all, but when I heard she was coming to stay with Aunt Zehra, I rushed to the airport to meet her. All her grandchildren living in Istanbul came too. Zehra's children, Ercan, Ersan and Emrah, brought their wives and children along. When she was brought out from the plane in a wheelchair, she looked tired, worn out.

There wasn't even an argument about which car she should ride in. Everything had to be as my grandmother wished. Because she liked the way Emrah drove, we put her into his car. Her daughters went with her. The rest of us followed in the other cars. Emrah took her up the apartment stairs in his arms. She seemed to be asleep. Had she been herself, she would have turned to Emrah and said, 'My boy, I'm begging you. You'll hurt your back.' Instead she opened her mouth like a bird a few times, but she couldn't manage a word.

We put her into bed, waiting for her to recover before we kissed her hand. A while later, she got up. We went to her each in turn, kissing her hand and trying to tell her who we were. She returned the kisses of all those who kissed her hand but recognised none of us. Our efforts to help her remember us were in vain.

After a time she recognised Emrah, and asked after his son Aydın. Encouraged to see her acknowledge Emrah, most of us went back and tried again; but still my grandmother couldn't recognise us.

My niece's wedding: my grandmother putting a bracelet onto the arm of the girl who would make her a *toruntaht*.

Then I went to her side. As always, I took her hands inside mine and said:

'Grandmother.' And she answered as she always did. 'Grandmother.' Then Aunt Sabahat, who was sitting next to her, leaned over to whisper into her ear: 'Look, Mother, look who's come!' My grandmother's reply was short and clear:

'I recognise her from her voice . . .'

I bit my lip to keep from crying and, burying my head in her hands, I kissed them. Then she kissed me. Still holding on to my hands, she asked me if I was well, and how work was going, and then: 'How is Gülçin?'

Gülçin was not a relative; she was a friend of mine. The others in the room looked at each other in surprise. This aged mind had to struggle to remember children and grandchildren, but here she was, able to recall someone she had not seen in a very long time.

Upon hearing that Gülçin was well, she then asked the question that would cause her family to burst into surprised laughter:

'How is her dog, is it still alive?'

Then she asked me a few more questions about what I'd been doing. But after she heard one answer, it would take her a bit of time to ask a second question. I think she was having trouble gathering her thoughts. Before long, she wanted to put her head on a pillow and lay down to rest.

I went back to see my grandmother the next day, and as often as I could thereafter. Every time I saw her, her condition had deteriorated. According to my aunt, she woke up only to eat and use the toilet.

When she heard me say, 'Grandmother,' she would still sit up and say, 'Grandmother'; she would hold my hand, but wouldn't be able to speak; tiring quickly, she would soon have to lie down. The last time I saw her, she was in bed. I went to her side and said, 'Grandmother.' She raised her head at once and took my hand, but she couldn't speak, couldn't even say 'Grandmother,' couldn't even hold up her head; she held onto my hand but once her head had fallen back into the pillows, she couldn't raise it again.

My grandmother and I never spoke again. She could no longer tell me about her village or her childhood or her handsome uncle who had worked as a teacher in Kiğı or her grandfather or her mother. No longer take my hands in hers and lose herself in her thoughts. She could no longer look up, and after fixing her gaze on a point in the ceiling, ask: 'In that courtyard of ours, there was something round. What was it, I wonder?' And she could no longer give me an answer.

I gave her death announcement to the newspaper *Agos*:[13]

Her name was Heranuş. She was the granddaughter of Herabet Gadaryan, and the only daughter of İsguhı and Hovannes Gadaryan.

She passed a happy childhood in the village of Habab, near Palu, until she reached the fourth grade.

Then suddenly, she was thrown into the painful times about which she would say, 'May those days vanish never to return'.

Heranuş lost her entire family and never saw them again. She was given a new name, to live in a new family.

She forgot her mother tongue and her religion, and though she did not once in her life complain about this, she never ever forgot her name, her village, her mother, her father, her grandfather or her close relations. She lived until the age of 95, always hoping that she might be able to see them and embrace them again one day. Perhaps it was this hope that allowed her to live so long; until her very last days, her mind remained sharp. Last week, we lost Heranuş, our grandmother, and sent her to her eternal resting

13 The Turkish-Armenian weekly that was edited by Hrant Dink until his assassination in January 2007.
Author's note: I gave the names in this notice as my grandmother had requested.

place. We are hoping that this announcement might reach the relations (our relations) that we were never able to find while she was alive, that they may share our grief, in the hope that 'those days may vanish, never to return.'

If I happen to find myself in the Istanbul district of Kadıköy and am not in a hurry, I always make sure to visit Hasan's bookstore. Hasan grew up in Maden, too. The older generations of our two families were well acquainted and on good terms. Hasan and I met in Istanbul and quickly became friends. After my grandmother had died, I dropped by to see him; as always, he ordered me a coffee with no sugar. I told him about my grandmother, and he expressed his sorrow and offered his condolences. As usual, we were soon deep in conversation.

At one point, he said, 'Do you know, when I was little, I came with my grandmother to your house. Your grandmother had made a *çörek*.[14] We stayed for a while, and after we'd eaten the *çörek*, went to visit Auntie Seher, Şaşo İbrahim's wife, and Auntie Tadımlı. I noticed that in every house we visited that day, we were offered the same *çörek*. And the *çörek*s in the other houses were sweet braided breads, just like yours, and decorated with eggs and dried cherry powder and fennel seeds, just like yours.

Of course I wanted each treat to be different, so I was disappointed when we kept getting offered the same *çörek*, but my grandmother ate a slice of *çörek* at each house we visited, and drank a glass of tea. It was only years later that I realised what all these houses we visited had in common. Auntie Seher, Şaşo

14 A braided sweet bread.

İbrahim's wife, was Armenian; Auntie Tadımlı was a Muslim convert, like your grandmother.'

I was shocked. I asked Hasan if he could recollect when these visits had taken place, but he couldn't remember exactly. But he recalled the visits themselves very clearly, and years later had seen what the houses where he'd eaten the *çörek*s had in common. Yes, my grandmother loved to make us sweet braided breads decorated with eggs and dried cherry powder and fennel seeds, and she would offer them to her guests, but I'd had no idea there were other households in Maden where women who shared similar pasts had made *çörek*s to give to visitors.

I realised now the significance of the *çörek* that our Armenian neighbours, Aznif Hanım and Yıldız Hanım, offered to their guests at Easter.

After we had shared what we knew, what we remembered, we were both overcome by emotion; tears welled up in our eyes. They might have hidden it from their children and grandchildren, but these women had carried on their traditions in secret; they'd not forgotten their holy days, and would visit their neighbours and celebrate together. It had taken until today to see this.

During a later visit, Hasan told me that people in the town had referred to my grandmother and others like her as 'the leftovers of the sword'. They'd be talking about someone, and they'd say, 'That one was a leftover of the sword, too.'

I felt my blood grow cold. I had heard this term before, but it wounded me to hear it used to describe my grandmother and those like her. The optimism that our memories of the *çörek*s had brought us gave way to dark thoughts.

Several months had passed when Hrant Dink rang one day from *Agos*: 'Can you come to the office? Your relatives from America are on the phone.'

When Hrant rang I was outside in the street, and it was raining. I have no memory of the conversation we went on to have, neither can I remember how it ended; I just stood there in the street, dumbstruck.

The death announcement I had given to *Agos* was later printed in a newspaper called *Haraç*, which was printed in France, alongside a news item that was critical of it. Archbishop Mesrob Aşçıyan, himself from the village of Habab, happened to notice it. A distant relation of the Gadaryans, Aşçıyan decided to ring them, and got through to Margaret, my grandmother's sister – the one who was born in America, the one whose face she'd never had a chance to see.

It was Richard Bedrosyan – Margaret's son, and my grand-mother's nephew – who rang *Agos*. I began to exchange letters with Margaret and Richard. Margaret (Auntie Marge, as she was known) wrote me the story of what had happened to İsguhı after she had been separated from her daughter. From her I learned that only two women from that large family had come through the death march alive, and that when they had reached Aleppo, they had been close to dying of starvation. These two women were İsguhı and her sister Diruhi. All the others – the grandmothers,

grandchildren, daughters and daughters-in-law who had set off on
the march with them – had lost their lives along the way, and their
bodies had been left by the side of the road.

Margaret also wrote to me that when her father had died in
1965, they'd found a piece of paper folded up in his wallet. This
letter that he'd folded and kept in his wallet for so many years was
from Heranuş. Margaret had saved it, and sent me a photocopy. I
invited both the American and Turkish branches of our family to
visit my grandmother Heranuş's grave together.

Baby Ege, who had made my grandmother a *toruntaht*, grew up without ever knowing her. One day, when this baby's own grandmother, Handan, was trying to put him to sleep, she told him the story of Sister Pizez. And she told the child that the story came from her grandmother's grandmother. Because they lived in different cities, Ege did not see his own grandmother again for a year. The next time they were together, Ege asked for a story.

'What story would you like? What tale should I tell you?' asked his grandmother.

In an eager voice, Baby Ege answered:

'Grandma, can you tell me the story of Sister Pizez?'

In 1910, following in the footsteps of his older brothers Boğos and Stepan, Hovannes went to Bremen, where he boarded a ship to America. But he was refused entry into the US. After this failed attempt, Hovannes tried to enter the United States via Canada; this time he succeeded. The three brothers worked together in the grocery store they owned together.

Later on, Hovannes opened his own grocery store on Tenth Avenue. He worked day and night, saving as much as he could. Before long, the terrible news reached him. He heard that there were no longer any Armenians in the lands they'd left behind, that only a few of the Armenians who'd been forced out of their villages had reached Aleppo and Der Zor[15], that almost everyone had been slaughtered – women and children, old and young – and that there were now campaigns to help the survivors, who were on the verge of death from starvation and neglect. The brothers went half mad. They knocked on every door but could find no news of their family. Some time later, the Red Cross began to publish lists naming the survivors. So now they began to visit the Red Cross, until Hovannes finally discovered that his wife was alive and in Syria. It was not until 1920 that he and İsguhı were reunited. They threw their arms around each other and cried, mourning the children and loved ones they had lost.

15 Also known as Dayr az-Zwar, the town was established by the Ottomans in 1867 and became part of independent Syria in 1946. Today it has a memorial to the Armenian victims of the death marches.

In 1928, when Hovannes discovered that Heranuş and Horen were still alive, he went straight to Aleppo. He paid a huge sum to some smugglers who worked the border, asking them to find his children and bring them to him. For days, for months, he watched the road they had left on. In the end, he found Horen. When Horen was brought to him, the first thing he did was to ask Horen to take off his shirt. When he saw the burn marks on his left shoulder and chest, Hovannes threw his arms around his son and for a long time he wept.

In America İsguhı and Hovannes had two more children, a son and daughter, Harold and Margaret.

When Margaret reached school age, they sent her to an Armenian school at the weekends so that she would learn the language. At the end of the first day, she ran home and, all out of breath, began to sing the Armenian song they had just learned at school. Expecting her mother to be glad, Margaret was surprised to see her crying. She stopped singing the song, because her mother had fallen to the floor and was sobbing. When she saw that she had frightened her little daughter, stunning her into silence, İsguhı explained why she had cried. The song Margaret had learned in school that day was Heranuş's favourite song, which she had sung most often.

When Hovannes died in 1965 aged eighty-six, Margaret found in his wallet, which he kept in his left breast, an old piece of paper folded into four. Fearful that she might tear it, she opened it with care: it was a letter written in Armenian, and there was writing on both sides. Heranuş had written on one side of the sheet, Maryam on the other. The paper was close to disintegrating so Margaret put it away in a safe place.

Margaret had trouble with her eyes. One day, when she was about to go into hospital for an eye operation, she got a call from Archbishop Mesrob Aşçıyan. He'd read about Heranuş's death in *Agos*. She rang her children at once. Richard, Nancy and Debra set out together to find the granddaughter who had placed the announcement.

We made contact; we began to write to each other. We exchanged photographs. Ayşe did the translations. Margaret went to church with her sons and daughters-in-law and her grand-children to pray for her husband, her father, her mother, and for Heranuş, too. Nancy, Heranuş's niece, arranged for ten trees to be planted in Armenia in her aunt's memory. Margaret was receiving the same treatment for her eye trouble as the older sister whose face she never had a chance to see. The operation was unsuccess-ful and, despite further surgery, her condition worsened, as did her asthma. Margaret was eighty years old and the doctors would not let her make the long journey to see her sister's grave. 'It doesn't look as if I'll ever make it to Heranuş's grave,' she told her children. 'And I'm going to die without seeing Fethiye.' Richard, Nancy and Debra decided to give her a surprise on her eightieth birthday.

When Ayşe called me her voice was once again shaking with excitement. 'Would you like to be the present at Margaret's eightieth birthday?'

Richard, Nancy and Debra met me at New York's JFK Airport. The reunion affected us all deeply. When Richard and I walked towards each other – it was more of a run than a walk – we both began to cry. We threw our arms around each other and began to wail. They'd told Margaret at the very last minute. Though she had only just got out of hospital, she came to meet me; after a five-hour drive, she'd had to spend hours waiting at the airport. They'd also invited Ayşe, who now lived in another part of the country; it took her six hours to fly to New York. Richard's wife Beth was also there. Our emotional reunion seemed to have made an impression on the people nearby; when we looked around we saw we had attracted a crowd of onlookers.

From the day the invitation arrived until the moment we met at the airport, I had been tense and anxious. Though we came from the same family, we were people who had grown up in different lands, speaking different languages and belonging to different cultures. I kept asking myself how it would be when we met: whether we would warm to each other, whether we would even be able to understand each other. I didn't close my eyes once during the flight. When I passed through passport control and customs I noticed that I was wet with perspiration. Moisture was streaming down my neck. But I tried to stay calm by reminding myself that Ayşe would be there. I saw her as my saviour. The moment I walked through the door, I heard a woman's soft voice, to my left on the other side of the iron partition, calling my name. When I turned my head I saw that it was Beth approaching me, with a smile that was as warm as her voice. We recognised each other from the photographs. Without waiting until we had reached the end of the partition separating new arrivals from those greeting them, we threw our arms around each other. Aunt Marge was right next to her. As we cried and embraced, she touched my neck and said, 'This is our family trait. This family perspires at the nape of the neck.' Our laughter mixed with our tears, and from that moment on all my anxieties left me, and I relaxed.

The same day, we went to New Jersey to visit my grandmother's parents' grave. I wanted to buy flowers, but it was early evening and most florists were shut. Of the flowers I was able to find, the best were pink roses, and I bought two bouquets: Hovannes and İsguhı were buried in the same grave. As I put the roses on the gravestone, I asked for absolution from my grandmother and all her family, in my name and in the names of those who had brought about their unspeakable pain.

Like her older sister, Auntie Marge loved to cook and entertain visitors. We ate royally throughout our time together, and conversed for hours on end. At every opportunity we wrapped our arms around each other and cried. Auntie Marge would take me by the hand and, grasping it tightly and gesturing upwards, she would try to console me by saying, 'She can see us, and believe me, she is overjoyed.'

I gave Marge a silk embroidered cloth and a loofah that my grandmother had made with her own hands. She held them as if she were afraid of hurting them. She unfolded them and turned them over in her hands, then folded them carefully, only to unwrap and caress them again. And all the while she moaned audibly. We were all there with her – Richard, Beth, Nancy, Debra, Debra's husband Michael, Ayşe and myself. As if by a prearranged signal, we all drew back, so that she could be alone with her older sister, retreating to the far side of the sitting room to grieve in our own way.

I had so many questions to ask Marge. To remind myself, I'd take notes at night, and every time I had the chance, would deluge her with questions. The person who got worn out during our visit was Ayşe, who was translating around the clock. The questions weren't all one-way. There was so much that Marge and my cousins wanted to learn from me, too.

One morning in the kitchen, after breakfast, Auntie Marge said, 'Heranuş's favourite song went like this,' and she began to hum it. She could remember the tune, but not the words. Try as she might, she could only remember the second line: 'played a song of love.' Suddenly I remembered the only song I'd ever heard my grandmother hum, during the days after I had told her I'd re-established contact with her brother. Now I asked myself if this was the song she had been humming. I shared my thoughts with Aunt Marge. She stopped, thought, and said, 'It could be.'

Marge tried very hard to remember the other words, but to no avail. She rang a few childhood friends, who couldn't remember either. But Aunt Marge didn't give up. She rang her church choir. Two women in the choir remembered the song, which was about a shepherd.

Hingalla[16]

A sad shepherd on the mountain
Played a song of love

A song for flaming cheeks
A song for burning eyes
A song for joyful days to come

Oh poor shepherd boy
Forever you will roam
The deep gorges and valleys

Hingalla, hingalla
A song for flaming cheeks
A song for burning eyes
A song for joyful days to come

16 Translated into English by Nouritza Matossian and Hagop Varoujian.

Here comes the springtime
Bringing fresh flowers
Bright coloured flowers
I love them 'hah hah hah'
Bright coloured flowers

Oh poor shepherd boy
Forever you will roam
The deep gorges and valleys
Hingalla, hingalla
A song for flaming cheeks
A song for burning eyes
A song for joyful days to come

'My mother never missed the village dances: she loved to dance, and she did so beautifully. But after her ordeal, she never danced again,' Aunt Marge told me afterwards. I asked her if she knew the dances. 'I do,' she said. I asked her if she would mind showing me a few steps. She didn't disappoint me. Leaning against the table, she rose to her feet. 'This is called the *halay*,' she said, and she began to dance. I sprang from my chair, ran to her side, put my arm in hers and together in her kitchen we did the *halay*.

The day before we parted company, the family gathered for a farewell meal. At one point during the meal Richard said, 'I must have been four or five years old when I first heard what the Turks had done to the Armenians. All my life, I've been afraid of Turks. I nurtured a deep hatred of them. Their denial has made things even worse. Then I found out that you were part of our family but Turkish at the same time. Now I love all parts of this big family and I'm desperate to meet my other cousins and even make music with them. But I still hate all those who deny what happened; these people I shall never forgive.'

*   *   *

Aunt Marge bought presents for my sister, brother, nieces and nephews. As she gave them to me, she said, 'I want so much to see them. But my health is getting steadily worse, and it's possible that I'll never have chance to do so – I hope they will think of me when they receive these.' She bought them all elegant presents that would last, accompanying each one with a handwritten note.

Then she said, 'We're family, too,' and wished that all of us, who had been separated for so long, would stay in touch from then on. Together we made this promise, and then we raised our glasses in a toast to every living member of our family.

A note on the author

Fethiye Çetin was born in Ergani-Maden. She attended schools in Mahmudiye, Maden, and Elazığ. A graduate of the Ankara University Law Faculty, and a member of the Istanbul Bar Association and the Committee to Promote Human Rights, she has also served as a spokesperson for the Minority Rights Working Group. Her articles have appeared in many newspapers and periodicals. She lives in Istanbul.

Printed in the United States
by Baker & Taylor Publisher Services